UFOs

TELEPORTATION, AND THE MYSTERIOUS
DISAPPEARANCE OF MALAYSIAN AIRLINES
FLIGHT #370

Robert Iturralde

BALBOA.PRESS

A DIVISION OF HAY HOUSE

Balboa Press books may be ordered through booksellers or by contacting:

Balboa Press
A Division of Hay House
1663 Liberty Drive
Bloomington, IN 47403
www.balboapress.com
844-682-1282

Because of the dynamic nature of the Internet, any web addresses or links contained in this book may have changed since publication and may no longer be valid. The views expressed in this work are solely those of the author and do not necessarily reflect the views of the publisher, and the publisher hereby disclaims any responsibility for them.

The author of this book does not dispense medical advice or prescribe the use of any technique as a form of treatment for physical, emotional, or medical problems without the advice of a physician, either directly or indirectly. The intent of the author is only to offer information of a general nature to help you in your quest for emotional and spiritual well-being. In the event you use any of the information in this book for yourself, which is your constitutional right, the author and the publisher assume no responsibility for your actions.

Print information available on the last page.

ISBN: 978-1-9822-7580-8 (sc)
ISBN: 978-1-9822-7581-5 (e)

Balboa Press rev. date: 10/13/2021

CONTENTS

INTRODUCTION

*"The most incomprehensible thing about the
Universe is that it is comprehensible."*
—Albert Einstein (3/14/1879–4/18/1955)

The disappearance of Malaysian Airlines Flight #370 is the major aviation mystery of the twenty-first century. I can only compare it to the disappearance of Flight #19 on 12-5-1945. I believe there are only two ways material objects disappear—natural and supernatural. My theory is that the intelligence behind the UFO phenomenon snatched the plane out of the air. I will examine every possible human factor in the disappearance of Flight #370. I will compare it to see if there is any similarity. The disappearance of Flight #370 is baffling because in cases of teleportation, the plane disappears completely. In the case of Flight #370, it seems that it was taken on a joyride of four to five hours. Also, there is the claim that some parts of the plane had been found. I will examine that claim.

My hope is that the plane will be found for the peace of the families of the passengers of the plane.

CHAPTER I

UFOs and Cases of Teleportation of Planes

"We all know that UFOs are real. All we need to ask is where do they come from?"

—Capt. Edgar D. Mitchell, Apollo 14
Astronaut, 1971 (9/17/1930–2/2016)

C*ase (1): The teleportation of Flight #19 in the Bermuda Triangle.* On December 5, 1945, five planes disappeared on a routine training mission. Flight #19 had a crew of five officer pilots and nine-crew members, two to each plane. The planes were Navy Grumman TB M-3 Avenger Torpedo bombers, and each carried enough fuel totravel 1,000 miles. The weather was beautiful, with sunshine and no clouds. Flight #19 left their base at Fort Lauderdale at 2:00 P.M. Lieutenant Charles Taylor, with over 2,500 hours of flight, was the commander. After training at about 3:15 p.m., the planes continued east. Further, the radioman at Fort Lauderdale Naval Air Station Tower received a call from Lt. Taylor. The records show the following:

> *Flight Leader Lt. Taylor:* Calling tower, this is an emergency. We are off course. We cannot see land. Repeat, we cannot see land.
> **Tower:** What is your position?

Lt. Taylor: We are not sure of our position. We cannot be sure just where we are. We seem lost.
Tower: Assume bearing due west.
Flight Leader Lt. Taylor: We don't know which way is west. Everything is wrong...strange. We can't be sure of any direction. Even the ocean doesn't look as it should.

About 3:30 p.m., the senior flight instructor at Fort Lauderdale picked up a message from someone calling Powers, one of the student flyers, requesting information about his compass readings. Powers answers, "I don't know where we are. We must have gotten lost after that last run." The senior flight instructor contacted the Flight #19 instructor, who told him, "Both my compasses are out. I am sure I am in the Keys, but I don't know how far down." The senior flight instructor advised him to fly further north. The gyro and magnetic compasses in all the planes were going crazy, showing different readings. After that, the powerful transmitter at Fort Lauderdale was unable to make contact with any of the planes. The personnel at the base were very worried and they began a search. So they sent a twin-engine Martin Mariner Flying Boat patrol with a crew of thirteen men from the Banana River Naval Station. Further, the Martin Mariner reported strong winds. According to official records, this was the last message received from the Flying Boat patrol with a crew of 13 men.

Immediately, a message was sent to all the search planes that there were now six planes missing. The next day one of the greatest searches ever in American his- tory took place. The search and rescue of the six planes involved 307 planes, four destroyers, eighteen Coast Guard boats, several submarines, search and rescue cutters, hundreds of private planes, yachts, boats, and additional PBMs from the Banana River Air Naval Station, also help from the RAF and Royal Navy units. The search included a daily average of 167 flights, flying about 300 feet above the water from morning to night. The search covered 380,000 square miles of land and sea, including the Atlantic, Caribbean, parts of the Gulf of Mexico, and Florida. Further, the air search completed 4,100 hours. The beaches of Florida and the Bahamas were searched daily for several weeks without success.

Moreover, no floating devices, no rafts, wreckage, or oil slick were found. Interestingly, during the search for Flight #19, witnesses reported UFOs—lights in red, green, and white described as *streaking or dancing* were seen from as far as the Keys to the Atlantic Ocean off Jacksonville. The same phenomenon is reported now before or after the disappearance of a plane or people. Flight #19 seemed to be lost in perfect weather. The reason is that the intelligence behind the UFO phenomenon can change human surroundings or the mental ability to see reality. That makes it easy for UFOs to kidnap planes and people.

I would like to mention that teleportation can take place with- out the physical presence of a UFO because the intelligence behind the UFO phenomenon has a super advanced technology that is beyond our imagination. The closest that I can imagine is that the UFO intelligence is somewhere in the universe, manipulating the basic structures of nature at the quantum (physics) level. Moreover, I want to describe the following events because they can help us to explain the disappearance of Flight #370. And then I will continue with the planes' disappearance.

Case (2): During the heat of the Cold War, in the early spring of 1966, UFOs were seen in the plains of Great Falls, Montana, Wyoming. In Great Falls, there are centers in buildings for nuclear deterrence in case of nuclear war. The missile combat crew commander Jack Davis and his fellow operator routinely entered one of the buildings and descended 60 feet into the underground launch control center, one of two reinforced capsules that contained equipment necessary for the control of ten missiles in separate under- ground launching facilities. After relieving their counterparts, Jack and the rest of the officers sat down before the command and status consoles. However, this night was not an ordinary night because, suddenly, one by one, ten lights blinked in imperfect sequence across the status console. The lights indicated that a fault existed in each of the ten assigned missiles simultaneously. The missile crew, in dis- belief, responded and electronically cleared each launch facility to determine the situation. In each case, the answer that automatically flashed back on the status console indicated a No Go fault condition. The signification of this event is that not one of the assigned missiles could be launched! Nothing like this ever happened before. Moreover, each fault was traced to the guidance and control systems, the most sophisticated and protected components of the Minuteman missile defense. Further, telephone communications revealed a frightening coincidence— above ground personnel had reported UFOs precisely during the failure of the ten missiles in the airspace.

Moreover, during the week of March 20, 1966, in another Minuteman base, a full set of ten missiles became inoperative; radar con- firmed a UFO and armed jet fighters were sent to intercept. Nonetheless, a missile program supervisor claimed that UFOs seriously endangered national security, although the Air Force denied this. As a matter of fact, Raymond E. Fouler, UFO scholar and project supervisor of a Minuteman missile program near Boston, claimed that UFOs have penetrated the restricted air space above America's Minuteman missile sites, jamming vital electronic equipment. He also said that UFOs eluded fighter jets sent to scramble and intercept them. Similarly, on August 25, 1966, in another missile base, radar operators picked up a UFO maneuvering over the base at 5,000 feet. The officer in charge declared that the LCF's sophisticated radio equipment, which enables it to receive firing instructions from coordinating centers and transmit them to the silo launch facilities, was blocked out by static when the UFO hovered directly over the base. The officer of the base said he could conceive of nothing on Earth that could cause the equipment to malfunction from such an altitude, that it was working perfectly before the UFO appeared overhead, and after the UFO left, the equipment worked fine.

Case (3): I would like to mention these two following cases because it may help us to solve the mystery of Flight #370. Further, we will continue with a long list of planes that had vanished. These are two cases of car kidnapping.

On December 12, 1967, a female was driving along Route 34 to her home in Ithaca, New York. Suddenly, she noticed that she was being followed by a red light. Her five-year-old son was also in the car. Mrs. Malley at first thought that a police car was signaling her to stop, but when she prepared to stop, she saw that the light was part of a disc-shaped UFO. The UFO was flying above the road to the left of her car. Afterward, in amazement and horror, she discovered that somehow the UFO was controlling her car. Mrs. Malley, frightened, called to her son, but he remained motionless in his seat, as some- thing was controlling his mind. She said, "It was as if he were in some kind of trance." Also, she reported, "The car pulled over to the shoulder of the road by itself, ran over an embankment into an alfalfa field, and stopped. Then a white twirling beam of light flashed down from the UFO, and I heard this humming sound. Then I began to hear voices. They didn't sound like male or female voices, but were weird. The words were broken and jerky, like the way a translator sounds when he is repeating a speech at the United Nations. But it was like a weird chorus of several voices. I became hysterical. My son wouldn't respond to my cries. I knew the radio wasn't turned on. The voices named someone I knew and said that at that moment my friend was involved in some terrible accident miles away. Also, they said my son would not remember any of this. Then the car began to move again, though still not under my control. We came out of that field and over the ditch as if it were nothing, and then back on the road." The voices had told the truth. Mrs. Malley heard the next day that a close friend had been involved in an automobile accident the night before. Mrs. Malley suffered from sobbing fits for days after the incident.

Case (4): A car intent of kidnapping by a UFO in the 1970s. A couple, Peter and Frances, reported the following experience to UFO researchers. "About six or seven miles south of Umuma, we spotted a figure sitting on a bank at the side of the road. It looked like a police- man or traffic officer speaking into a walkie-talkie. We suspected a speed trap. The figure had a curious metallic look. Neither of us thought of it at the time—2:15 in the morning on a remote stretch of a road—as an unlikely place for a speed trap. About a quarter of an hour later, I glanced out of my window to the left and I saw light which I thought must be coming from a house on top of a hill. Then I realized that it was too high up for this and was revolving. We were not much concerned, thinking in terms of a helicopter or some kind of beacon. Gradually, the light seemed to get closer to us and it was keeping pace with the car. Then the car lights were beginning to fade. By now, the UFO was above us and slightly to the left. The failure of the car lights didn't matter, though, for the UFO was giving off enough light to shine up the road ahead and cast shadows. It was like driving under a huge neon light. It slowly dawned on me that I'd completely lost control of the Peugeot. We were gaining speed. So I took my foot off the accelerator. Nothing happened. I gingerly depressed the brake pedal. There was no reaction from the power brake. Then I thought, let's try the steering wheel. It turned right but the car didn't. I was petrified. Frances had noticed some of my maneuvers but had not realized their implications. She asked me how I could be so calm. I didn't try to explain. But I didn't experiment again with the controls. I just hoped they had somehow come right on their own. Meanwhile, we were rushing along the narrow road, taking the turns perfectly, without any help from me. The interior of the car had fallen sharply in temperature, from the mid-eighties to low fifties."

Peter and Frances pulled on extra jerseys. The couple continued with their story. Further, the couple saw the UFO that had been following them for nearly two hours disappear like a shooting star over the horizon, and Peter found himself in control of the car again. A couple of miles later, they found a gasoline station. Peter said, "My only emotion as I switched off the engine was 'Thank God, it is all over,' I said to Frances." Peter then checked the car over. He switched the lights on and off. He said, "As best I could under the circumstances, I checked the electrical system, the headlights, the fuses and wiring, the ignition, the steering, and the brakes. I couldn't fault any- thing nor understand why the car had not behaved normally before." "The distance from Fort Vic to the border is about 150 miles. A few minutes outside Fort Vic, something made us look up. A UFO appeared as if from nowhere. There was just a light in the sky which again kept pace with the car," said Frances.

Again, Peter and Frances were shocked to find themselves with- out control of the car. Peter said, "I was shocked to find that once again I had no control of the car and the car was gathering speed. The car was going over 100 miles per hour. The normal top speed was around 70 miles per hour." Peter proceeded with their story. "I knew we were traveling with- out control at an impossibly high speed, but I was hardly reacting. I felt as if I were in a coma and found it difficult to keep track of time. At about 6:15 a.m., it got gradually lighter. But there was no sign of the sun itself. What have they done with the sun?" The UFO was still overhead after Frances drifted off to sleep. They traveled another one hour and fifteen minutes to the border while Frances slept. Peter can't remember what happened to them during this period. The UFO was still above the car.

"As we were looking, suddenly, it was gone. The next surprise came when we filled up the car for the next leg of the journey. We'd just traveled nearly 200 miles. Yet when the petrol attendant started to pump fuel, we needed less than a quarter of a gallon." Peter then checked the trip counter which he had set at zero in Fort Victoria. Peter said, "It registered just over 10 miles." They had driven to the Beit Bridge, apparently, for about two hours while the UFO hovered above. They had used no fuel and added no miles to the indicator. No explanation for this was forthcoming until the hypnosis sessions. Peter and Frances contacted Paul Obertick, who uses hypnotism in his medical practice.

> *Dr. Paul:* You were traveling twelve kilometers from Fort Victoria. What happened then?
> *Peter:* We were twelve kilometers outside Fort Victoria when we saw a UFO above. It sent down two beams of light—I don't know what type they were—into the car which gave the car a complete mind of its own, its own sense of power, direction, speed, control, steering ability, lighting, everything. At one stage, the car was telling me what to do—smoke a cigarette, light the lighter, change the radio setting from Lourence Marques to another station.

After their experience, they suffered a constant depression.

Case (5): On September 10, 1971, a Phantom II Sting 27 jetfighter was on a routine mission out of Homestead Air Force Base, south of Miami. The jet took off at 8:05 a.m. and its last radar return was at 8:22 a.m. Shockingly, there were other Phantoms and Coast Guard vessels in the area. Still, the jet fighter vanished without a trace. The area was searched with sonar but no trace of the fighter jet was ever found.

Case (6): On December 28, 1948, a DC-3 passenger plane chartered for a flight from San Juan, Puerto Rico, to Miami vanished within sight of Miami. The weather was excellent, the pilots were experienced, and there no signals of mechanical problems. The plane had twenty-seven passengers, including two infants. The captain of the plane contacted the Miami control tower, stating that they were approaching the field from fifty miles south and were waiting for landing instructions. Whatever happened to the DC-3 was fast and decisive—so fast that there was no time for a distress call. The tower sent the landing instructions but there was no response. The plane was almost within reach of the airport and simply vanished. A search and rescue was launched without luck. Again, no oil slick, no life jackets, and no wreckage or debris were found.

Case (7): On February 11, 1930, the Beech Baron 58 left St. Thomas in a short trip for Miami. The pilot's last message was that they were descending to ditch but were completely disoriented in a strange cloud. Nothing was ever heard of the pilots or plane. Nothing was found—no wreckage, debris, oil slick, or any floating device from the plane.

Case (8): The Kinross plane disappearance on November 23,1953. According to UFO researchers, the Air Force had only two sheets of paper about the disappearance of the plane. Obviously, this is a complete disregard of the truth—that the plane was snatched by a UFO. The reports of many investigators provided us with a clue about what happened to the plane. On the evening of November 23,1953, radars at Trax Air Force Base picked up an unidentified blip over restricted airspace. In fact, because the UFO was in a restricted area, an F-89 interceptor was scrambled from Kinross Field. Ground radar directed the jet flown by Lieutenant Felix Moncla Jr. toward the UFO. The people on the ground asked if the radar officer on theF-89 had the UFO on his scope. He answered "No," but they continued to track it on radar. The UFO, which had been hovering, accelerated as it headed out over Lake Superior, with ground controllers directing the jet. Lt. Felix Moncla raced after the UFO at over 500 miles per hour. The chase continued for nine minutes, with Moncla gaining slightly on the UFO. Further, the radar officer was able to get a fix on the target with the onboard radar. The distance narrowed and the jet closed in until it suddenly caught the UFO.

The military personnel on the ground watched in amazement how the two *blips* seemed to *merge*. At first, the military personnel didn't seem to be alarmed because they thought that the jet had flown under the UFO. However, the frightening thing is that the *blips* didn't separate. According to witnesses, "They hung there together for a short time, and then the single *blip flashed* off the radar screens." Moreover, attempts to reach Lt. Moncla on the radio failed. Eventually, the search and rescue units were given the last known position of the jet. Further, the search and rescue continued all night with the help of the Canadian Air Force. All the military personnel were sure that Lt. Moncla and the radar officer would survive because they carried enough equipment to survive a crash into the lake. Although a very good search and rescue team was organized after the plane disappeared, unfortunately, the search and rescue team didn't find an oil slick, no wreckage, and no bodies. The last trace of the F-89 was seen just as the two radar blips merged. Interestingly, after the F-89's disappearance, two fighter pilots reported that they were paced by a large, bright UFO.

Case (9): On October 30, 1954, Flight #441, a Lockheed four-engine Super Constellation airliner in military transport service was carrying forty-two passengers, all of them family of Navy service- men overseas. Everything indicated that the flight was normal with- out any emergencies. The pilot's messages were routine since he left from Maryland to Bermuda where it disappeared. The plane was carrying five life rafts, life jackets, forty-six exposure suits, pillows, and 660 paper cups. A very well-organized search and rescue took place, but there were no bodies, no wreckage, not even signs of its floatable cargo. The final conclusion of the Naval Board of Inquiry summarizes what is said of any missing airplane in the Bermuda Triangle: "It is the opinion of the board that the plane did meet a sudden and violent force that rendered the aircraft no longer airworthy, and was thereby beyond the scope of human endeavor to control. The force that rendered it uncontrollable is unknown."

Case (10): On October 14, 1961, a military aircraft, Pogo #22, an eight-engine Boeing B-52, was operating out of Seymour Johnson AFB in North Carolina, along with five other B-52s. Pogo #22 (its squadron name) was participating in *Sky Shield 11*, a secret Cold War maneuver for strike deterrent readiness. According to military officials, its return trip to base was a large arc extending from Nova Scotia to Bermuda. Further, while the six B-52s were in flight, they split up to a ten-mile lateral separation and headed west for base. Pogo #22 was last seen by its squadron about three miles away during the separation. The other five B-52s cruised into base on schedule, with the exception of Pogo #22. After officials learned that one of the B-52s was missing, an immediate search and rescue team was formed by Coast Guard cutters, Navy destroyers, cruisers, C-130 Hercules planes, and civilian vessels. The search and rescue mission covered 280,000 square miles of sea, roughly twice the area of California. Nevertheless, no wreckage, oil slick, or bodies were found of the B-52, even though this aircraft is 160 feet long, has a 186-foot wing- span, and is forty feet high. Shockingly, the airplane vanished within a very busy route, and only ten miles separated it from the rest of the squadron. Further, the Air Force reported that no explosion was heard, no Mayday; also, it was beautiful weather.

Case (11): In another case of teleportation, on October 31, 1991, a Grumman Cougar jet was being tracked on radar over the Gulf of Mexico. The pilot had just requested ascent from 23,000 feet to 29,000 feet. Radar tracked the aircraft during its climb until, for some unknown reason, it simply faded away. The radar readouts confirmed that the jet had not been captured as descending or falling to the sea; it simply disappeared in the air.

Case (12): The disappearance of the Cessna 402B Flight #201 twin engine. The charter plane was flying between Miami and Bimini on March 31, 1984. The plane carried six people. The aircraft was tracked on radar and nothing unusual was observed. Suddenly, the plane slowed to a very low speed of a mere 90 knots. According to personnel in the airport in Miami, they continued for approximately four minutes, without any indication from the pilots that something was wrong. Shockingly, the plane then plummeted in a 5,400 feet per minute dive until it vanished from radar. A clue to the fate of Flight #201 deepened. An eyewitness at Bimini reported seeing a plane plunge into the sea about one mile off the northeast corner of the island. Another reported seeing a huge splash in the ocean. Both witnesses mentioned a similar time—between 8:30 and 9:00 a.m. Further, all this information points that the aircraft disappeared at least thirty miles away from Bimini. Although the plane crashed in the ocean, it never reappeared on radar, and there had been no SOS or Mayday call from the pilots. Shockingly, the water in this area is only about eighteen feet deep. A search and rescue team found no wreckage, oil slick, or the bodies of the six people.

Case (13): The famous Gorman incident. This case is very famous in UFO history. On October 1, 1948, in Fargo, North Dakota, according to reports, the pilot, George F. Gorman, reported to the tower a light that he was following. The light was blinking on and off. Suddenly, the light became steady. Gorman followed and tried to get closer. The UFO appeared to try to ram the jet, and Gorman had to dive to get out of the way. The UFO passed over the jet's canopy only a few feet apart. Again the UFO and the F-51 jet turned and closed on each other head on. Again the pilot had to dive out to prevent a collision. All of a sudden the UFO began to climb and disappeared. After that, the pilot returned to base.

Case (14): On the night of October 18, 1973, a four-man Army Reserve crew was flying its helicopter over Mansfield, Ohio. The helicopter was cruising at about 2,500 feet when the UFO appeared. The crew was flying toward Cleveland when they spotted the UFO. The light appeared small and seemed to pace the helicopter. The pilot called the base in Mansfield for help to identify the light. The pilot had just made contact with the base when the communications system mysteriously malfunctioned and conked out. The crew began getting nervous, as the UFO began closing in on the helicopter. The UFO began growing larger and larger as it approached, moving right on a collision course. The crew panicked when they thought that the UFO was going to ram them. One of the crew members said, "This thing came out of nowhere and just stopped. It was like the hull of a dark submarine. The object hovered for several seconds, right outside the helicopter. I really didn't expect us to collide because the object was obviously in control of the situation. The edge was sharp because it was an exceedingly bright, starry night and the solid part of it blot- ted out the stars right behind it in an oval shape. The red light was affixed to a cigar-shaped, domed, and metallic spacecraft. A white light was shining from the rear of the ship, while a green light glowed from beneath it." As they watched in shock, the green light began revolving, as though surveying its victims, and then shot a beam of eerie light right into the helicopter and through its windows. Finally, the UFO flew away.

Case (15): On June 28, 1980, near the coast of Puerto Rico, the pilot of an Ercoupe reported that a weird object was in his flight path and was forcing him to change course despite all his evasive maneuvers. The object continued to cut him off. He reported his equipment was on the fritz and he was lost. He called "Mayday! Mayday," then astounded controllers watched the plane vanish from the screens. The plane disappeared. Minutes later, the UFO reappeared on the scope and disappeared from the screens. A search for the plane was launched but nothing was found. No wreckage, no oil slick, no bodies were found.

Case (16): On October 21, 1978, Frederick Valentich, a twenty- year-old pilot with the Australian Air Training Corps, left Moorabrin Airport in Victoria at 6:20 p.m. for King Island. His flight path would take him across the Bass Strait Triangle where planes disappeared and unexplained mechanical failures and magnetic anomalies occurred. Valentich was about forty-five minutes into his flight when he contacted the air tower near Melbourne about a speeding object which seemed on a collision course with his single-engine Cessna 182. According to tower controllers, the radar screen was clear. The control tower transcript goes like this:

Valentich: Melbourne, this is Delta Sierra Juliet (Valentich's call sign). Do you have any known traffic below 5,000 feet?

Tower: Delta Sierra Juliet, no known traffic. Valentich: I am seeing a large aircraft below 5,000. Tower: What type of aircraft is it?

Valentich: I cannot affirm. It is four bright lights. It seems to me like landing lights.

Tower: Delta Sierra Juliet?

Valentich: Melbourne, the aircraft has just passed over me, at least a thousand feet above.

Tower: And it is a large aircraft? Confirm.

Valentich: Unknown due to the speed it's traveling. Is there any aircraft from the Air Force in the vicinity?

Tower: No known aircraft in the vicinity.

Valentich: It's approaching now from due east toward me. It seems to me that he is playing some sort of game. He is flying over me two, three, at speeds I could not identify.

Tower: Confirm you cannot identify the aircraft.

Valentich: It's not an aircraft as it's flying past. It's a long shape, cannot identify more than that. It has such speed. It's before me right now. What I am doing is orbiting, and the thing is just orbiting on top of me. Also, it's got a green light and is sort of metallic, like it's all shiny on the outside. It's just vanished again.

Tower: Confirm the aircraft just vanished?

Valentich: It's now approaching from the southwest. The engine is idling rough. I've got it set at 2324 and the thing is coughing. That strange aircraft is hovering on top of me again. It's hovering and is not an aircraft!

Then a metallic sound was heard. This was the last transmission of Frederick Valentich. The day was beautiful. A search and rescue was organized for five days, twenty-four hours a day, and the daylight search continued for three weeks. No debris, oil slick, or body was found. His father still believes his son is alive.

Case (17): In 1953, during test flights from the local Russian military airfield over Kunashir Island, a jet vanished. Observers watched it on radar and visually. Ships were sent to search and found nothing. No wreckage, no oil slick, or no bodies.

Case (18): In 1982 in Byelorossia, a Mig-21 disappeared during a routine test flight in a militarized zone. UFOs were seen after the disappearance.

Case (19): In 1992 in Russia, radars were following the flight of the new Soviet SU-27 jet fighter plane when it suddenly vanished from the screens. The Russian air defense reported a UFO in the vicinity. A search followed for one month. However, no wreckage, oil slick, or bodies were found.

Case (20): Furthermore, the disappearance of a Cessna #402C on May 27, 1987 was bizarre. In this case, the plane was clearly seen to pass over its destination of Marsh Harbour, Great Abaco Island, and continue eastward as if the pilot had never seen his destination below. The plane was perfect without any trouble, and the large island was clearly visible in perfect weather. Nevertheless, no trace of the plane was ever found; no distress call was received.

Case (21): On June 3, 1987, a large Cessna #401 disappeared between Freeport, Grand Bahama, and Crooked Island with four persons. No trace of the plane or passengers was found.

Case (22): On December 2, 1987, a Cessna #152 disappeared in a short trip between Dominican Republic and San Juan, Puerto Rico.

Case (23): On January 24, 1990, another Cessna vanished on a short route during an instructional flight in perfect weather off the east coast of Florida. Although they were always in view of the coastal lights of West Palm Beach, the flight simply vanished without a trace. No Mayday or ELT device sent any signal.

Case (24): On Christmas 1994, a Cherokee, a small Piper, disappeared near Florida over land, last seen fighting power loss while flying over a house. In this last sighting, the pilot never reported a problem. The plane and pilot were never found.

Case (25): On May 12, 1999, an Aero Commander 500 per-formed some unexplained maneuvers before it vanished from radar near Nassau. The Cherokee Aero 500 was clocked by Nassau radar as steadily descending. However, the pilot never reported anything unusual. The radar then registered 000 altitudes, but thirty minutes later, he reappeared and requested to land at Nassau, did unusual maneuvers which angered the controller (though the pilot seemed unaware of them), then climbed to 1,300 feet where the plane completely vanished.

Case (26): The Mantell case. On January 7, 1948, just after 5:00 p.m., the search and rescue team found the wreckage of Captain Thomas Mantell's F-51 Mustang. He had crashed two hours earlier while chasing a UFO near Fort Knox, Kentucky. It was at 1:20 p.m. that the Godman Airfield tower crew sighted *a bright, disc-shaped object.* According to official Air Force records, the Kentucky Highway Patrol first reported the UFO, and it was quickly brought to the attention of the base operations officer, the intelligence, and finally the base commander, Colonel Guy F. Hoix. For an hour and twenty-five minutes, dozens of people, including Colonel Hix, watched the UFO as it hung almost motionless in the southwest-ern sky. In towns separated by more than 175 miles, people saw the UFO. Some claimed it drifted silently and slowly to the south, and others watched as it hovered for minutes before it resumed its slow flight. Conventional aircraft and helicopters were quickly dismissed. The object moved too slowly and quietly, and it was too bright. As a consequence, all other explanations were quickly eliminated. Further, the UFO was too large for any known balloons. At 2:25 P.M., a flight of F-51s flew over Godman Field. The UFO was still visible, and the flight commander, Thomas Mantell, was asked if he could investigate. He replied that he will attempt an intercept. He began a spiraling, climbing turn to 220 degrees and 15,000 feet. As the flight passed through 15,000 feet, two of the wingmen turned back. At that altitude, they were supposed to be on oxygen, but not all the aircraft were equipped with it and none had a full supply. The Air Force records show that the wingmen attempted to contact Captain Mantell but were unsuccessful. In the tower, they heard Captain Mantell's transmission. Mantell did say that the UFO was "above and ahead of me and appears to be moving about half my speed." Also, he said that it was metallic and "is tremendous in size." Finally, he said that the UFO was just above him and he continued to climb. The two other airmen turned back to the base. At 3:10 p.m., Captain Mantell was alone at 23,000 feet, still climbing and closing on the UFO. He made no further radio calls to either the tower or his wingmen. By 3:15 p.m., they had lost visual and radio contact with him. Immediately, search and rescue was launched. Just after 5:00 p.m. on a farm near Franklin, Kentucky, the remains of the F-51 were found splattered over half a mile. Mantell's body was inside the cockpit. The Air Force explanation is that the UFO was the planet Venus or weather balloons.

Case (27): In June 1953, an F-94C jet attempted to intercept a UFO near Otis AFB in Massachusetts when it failed to respond to radar identification. According to the pilot's sworn testimony, at an altitude of 1,500 feet over the base rifle range, the engine quit functioning and the entire electrical system failed. The pilot yelled to the radar operator (over the battery-operated intercom) to bail out and jettison the canopy because the aircraft was seconds from impact. The crippled plane should have crashed, but it wasn't there nor the radar operator. Only the pilot was found. Sergeant CD stated that "this incident caused one of the most extensive and intensive searches I have ever seen, for three months." The aircraft and the radar operator were never found. Shockingly, the jettisoned canopy was found within the confines of the rifle range.

Case (28): On January 5, 2007, an hour after Boeing 737 Adam Air Flight #K1-574 took off on New Year's Day with 102 passengers and crew for what should have been a short trip between islands, the pilot reported heavy winds, then the plane disappeared into thin air. No Mayday or distress calls were sent.

Case (29): On May 10, 2012, a Russian jet with fifty people vanished in Indonesia. a new Russian-made passenger plane over mountains in western Indonesia, while on a demonstration flight arranged for potential buyers. Search and rescue teams were deployed to the area, just south of the capital Jakarta. The super jet took off from the Halim Perdana Fusuma Airport at 2:21 p.m. for a quick test flight. After twenty-one minutes into the flight, the pilot asked air traffic control for permission to drop from 10,000 feet to 6,000 feet. They didn't explain the change of course. The weather was good. There were no signs of distress or Mayday calls. The cell phones of the passengers were either turned off or not active. The aircraft had gone through a preflight check without any technical problems. The plane was never found.

Case (30): In 2013, a twin-engine plane with eleven passengers left Santiago, Dominican Republic, with a flight plan to land in the Bahamas, but the plane never arrived. The pilot sent an emergency signal about thirty-five minutes after takeoff, and then the plane dis- appeared from radar. The Coast Guard searched without turning up any sign of the plane or its passengers. No oil slick, debris, or any floatable device from the plane.

Case (31): On December 3, 2005, a twin-engine plane piloted by George F. Baker III, a philanthropist, disappeared off the coast of Nantucket, Long Island. The search was called off after an eighteen-hour canvass by Coast Guard boats, planes, and divers. The plane, a Beech Baron Be #55, disappeared from radar at 4:45 p.m. at an altitude of 200 feet. The plane had already been cleared to land and did not send a distress signal or Mayday call. The Coast Guard stated, "No trace was found of the plane which was believed to have crashed one-mile south of the island." Newlin said the Coast Guard found *no signs, debris of Baker's plane*, although the police reported a red light in the water.

Case (32): On January 29, 1948, a big British four-engine air- liner named the Star Tiger radioed that it was on course 400 miles from Bermuda en route to Kingston with twenty-six passengers and crew members aboard. The weather was excellent and no trouble was reported by the pilot. No other message was received. A search and rescue team was organized but no wreckage, oil slick, or debris were found.

Case (33): On January 17, 1949, the Star Ariel left Bermuda for a trip to Kingston, Jamaica. The plane was carrying fuel for an extra ten hours of flight, just in case. Forty minutes after it left Bermuda, the captain radioed that the weather was fair; expected arrival at Jamaica on time. After that, only silence. Intensive search found no debris, oil slick, or bodies.

Case (34): In March of 1956, three US Air Force personnel disappeared over the Mediterranean Sea while flying a Boeing B-47 Stratojet long-range bomber. The plane was traveling from the MacDill Air Force Base in Florida en route to the Ben Gurion Air Force Base in Morocco as part of a four-plane flight. While three planes showed up at their aerial refueling point, one went missing and no wreckage, oil slick, or debris were found. The plane was carrying two nuclear weapons cores, and the people there were never found.

Case (35): In 1954 two US Navy propeller-driven planes, AD-6 Raiders attack planes, took off from Moffett Field on a routine flight of two hours to Fallon, Nevada. They never arrived. The Navy spokesman called the disappearance baffling and he added, "It is very strange that both planes have disappeared without a word from either to base." Immediately, thirteen aircraft searched all over the route they had taken. No signs, debris, oil slick, or bodies were ever found.

Case (36): On April 6, 1956, search and rescue teams looked over three states for a clue to the disappearance of a secret Lockheed jet plane on an experimental flight over Nevada. The plane was at high altitude in a test flight. The weather was good. Again, the plane disappeared without a trace. No debris, oil slick, or bodies were found. There were two crew members.

Case (37): On June 26, 1956, a jet fighter plane took off from Alameda Naval Air Station. The pilot flew into a bank of clouds and the plane was never seen again.

Case (38): In January 1949, a charter plane radioed that it was fifty miles from Miami, Florida, and that "All was well." Suddenly, it vanished without a trace. The plane carried thirty-three people. No wreckage, oil slick, or bodies were found.

Case (39): In the month of December 1949, nine planes vanished without a trace off the coast of Florida. No wreckage, oil slick, or bodies of 108 people from all nine planes were ever found.

Case (40): On August 12, 1947, the Star Dust vanished in three minutes after radioing that it was coming close to land. The last message was followed by a mysterious word STENDEC which has never been deciphered. The plane never was found; no debris, oil slick, or bodies.

Case (41): In the last week of January 1951, the Pan American Airliner Constellation, bound from Johannesburg to New York, radioed from somewhere in the Gulf of Guinea at 3:00 a.m. that it was ready to land on the Liberian Airfield. At 3:15 a.m., it suddenly vanished in the last fifteen minutes. The plane carried forty people. Immediately, twelve French planes took off from Dakar and were joined by British planes. However, after an exhaustive search and rescue, nothing was found—no debris, oil slicks, or bodies.

Case (42): On August 22, 1956, a medium US bomber being ferried from Iceland to France to be handed over to the French Air Force took off from Keflavik Air Base after dawn in perfect weather. Twenty minutes later, another US plane took off from the same base for France. The later plane got a message from the base control at Keflavik: "Get contact with the first plane. We can get no reply from her." The second plane called the first repeatedly but had no reply. The pilot said, "This was strange, for on a previous trip from the US, we were in constant radio contact. I cannot understand it." A rigorous search and rescue operation found nothing—no debris, wreck- age, or oil slick.

Case (43): In March 1957, a double-decker US military Strato Cruiser #C1927 vanished inexplicably, going from Travis Air Force Base in North

Carolina to Tokyo, Japan. For nine days, eleven American planes searched some thousands of square miles of the Pacific. Close to seventy planes took part in the search. The plane had sixty-seven passengers and crew. No debris, oil slick, or bodies were found.

Case (44): The disappearance and fate of Amelia Earhart. This is the most famous disappearance. Obviously, there are many stories, and it has become a modern myth. She and Noonan were flying a twin-engine Lockheed Electra. They took off from Lae, New Guinea, at 10:00 a.m. on July 2, 1937 in a trip to Howland Island in the mid-Pacific, a distance of 2,556 miles. During the later stages of the flight, the Electra's crew were in constant contact with the US Navy cutter *Itasca* stationed off Howland to provide the aircraft with navigational assistance. At 7:42 a.m. on July 3, the cutter received a radio transmission from Amelia Earhart. "We must be over you," she said. "We cannot see you. Gas running low. We are flying at an altitude of 1,000 feet." Sixteen minutes later, a further transmission was received. "We are circling you. We see you. We cannot hear you."

The *Itasca* answered, "Go ahead on 7500, either now or on scheduled time of half hour." The *Itasca's* radio operator transmit- ted a direction-finding signal on the arranged frequency of 7,500 kilocycles.

The Electra's pilot reported that she was receiving it but was unable to get a bearing. "Please take a bearing on us and answer by voice on 3105," she requested. The radio operator sent out voice transmissions at five-minute intervals. At 8:45 a.m. Amelia Earhart responded, "We are in line of position 157-337. We are running north and south. We are listening on 6210 kilocycles." That was the last transmission of Amelia. The crew of the *Itasca* thought that the Electra was off course and lost. They calculated that the aircraft might have enough fuel for another three hours of flying.

In the days following the Electra's disappearance, one of the greatest search and rescue efforts was organized, the *Itasca* leading the search with planes and ships, the search of 250 square miles of the central Pacific. Also looking for Amelia were an aircraft carrier, a battleship, four destroyers, a mine sweeper, as well as a half dozen small planes. Further, the aircraft carrier US *Lexington* launched sixty aircraft. In the next five days, they searched 151,000 square miles of the ocean, and no debris, oil slick, or bodies were found.

Interestingly, I see a similarity with Flight #19. It seems to me that in both cases the pilots seemed disoriented, even though the weather seemed fair. According to the records, Amelia said, "We are circling you. We cannot hear you." Also, she said, "We cannot see you. Gas running low." Likewise, Flight #19 seemed lost. The messages were, "We don't know which way is west. Everything is wrong…strange. We can't be sure of any direction." We see that the weather is clear and there is no mechanical reason for this behavior. My conclusion is that the intelligence behind the UFO phenomenon creates a mental blockade to kidnap the plane and pilot or pilots and crew, similarly in the next case.

Case (45): On May 27, 1987, a Cessna #402C disappeared. The plane was clearly seen to pass over its destination of Marsh Harbour, Great Abaco Island. It seemed that the pilot had never seen the destination a couple of hundreds of feet below. The pilot didn't report any problem with the plane, and the weather was fair. A search and rescue team found no wreckage, oil slick, or bodies. Similarly, Amelia couldn't see the Itasca. In the 1950s, General Benjamin Chidlaw, former head of US continental air defense, said, "We have lost too many men and planes trying to intercept them (UFOs)."

Case (46): In this case, the plane was not teleported, only one passenger. On June 29, 1968, Jerrold Potter and his wife were flying in a DC-3 with twenty-one other passengers. The weather was excellent, and the pilot did not report any problems. Mr. Potter was talking to everyone in the plane. His wife saw him walking to the lavatory. She never saw him again. She went to check the lavatory, but no sign of her husband. She asked the stewardess to check the lavatory. The check of the plane was total, but no signs of Jerrold Potter were found. Also, there were no signs that any emergency door had been opened. He disappeared; teleported.

CHAPTER II

UFO's and Cases of Teleportation in the Oceans

"Air Force, Navy and commercial pilots have revealed to me when a UFO would fly right off their plane's wing. Highly secret government investigations are going on that we don't know about."

—Senator Barry Goldwater
(1/2/1909–5/29/1998)

T he Indian Ocean is an enormous ocean which includes the Arabian Sea, the Bay of Bengal, the Timor Sea, and the South China Sea. The most prominent port cities are Kuala Lumpur, Jakarta, Rangoon, Zanzibar, Karachi, Bombay, Colombo, Muscat, etc. The Indian Ocean is 73,429,000 sq. km. or 28,351,000 sq. miles and an average depth of 3,840 miles or 12,598 feet. We seldom hear about the different weird phenomena that take place there. Also, in the Indian Ocean, there are very dangerous wildlife; for instance, the ferocious estuarine crocodile, the deadly sea snake, killer sharks, and many other species.

Case (47): For example, in February 1948, a number of ships picked up a distress signal coming from the eastern part of the Bay of Bengal. The SOS was from the Dutch freighter *Ourang Medan* in the Malacca Strait. The *Ourang Medan* had been bound for Jakarta, Indonesia. A rescue ship went to investigate, and a boarding crew found the officers and crew lying along the deck. All men were dead and according to the report, "Their eyes were open and glaring at the blazing sun Their outstretched arms, frozen in rigor mortis, were reaching toward the sky." Even the ship's dog was found dead, its face contorted in an *eternal snarl*. Shockingly, the bodies did not show any signs of violence or injury. A complete forensic check of the ship failed to find the cause of death of the crew of the *Ourang Medan*.

Case (48): On February 7, 1953, the British cargo ship *Ranne* was navigating the waters near the Bay of Bengal. The *Ranne's* look- out sighted an apparently abandoned vessel. A boarding party was sent to investigate. They discovered the table with the meals of the crew intact and fresh. The name of the ship was *Holchu*. The vessel had plenty of food, fuel, and provisions. Only the crew was missing, nowhere to be found. An investigation failed to find the reason for the crew to disappear.

Case (49): The great Danish ship *Kobenhann* set sail from Argentina bound for Australia with five dozen people aboard. Eight days later, as it traversed the South Atlantic, it radioed a nearby ship that all *seemed well*. This event took place on December 28, 1928. The ship was never heard from again. Associated Press correspondent Alex Gerfalk wrote, "Never in the history of shipping has a missing vessel been searched more thoroughly. Science has examined its resources in an attempt to find a plausible explanation for the complete disappearance of the largest sailing vessel in the world."

Case (50): On June 18, 2003, Frank and Romina Leone left Boynton Beach, Florida, in their sixteen-foot boat for a day excursion. They and their boat were never found. The Leones launched their boat on a Wednesday afternoon, and when the couple failed to show up at each of their jobs in West Palm Beach, family and friends were very worried. The Coast Guard launched a search and rescue mission which covered over 35,700 square miles from Miami to Savannah, Georgia. However, the boat and the couple were never found.

Case (51): On March 4, 1918, the USS *Cyclops*, a Navy fuel ship, left Barbados bound for Hampton Roads, Virginia. The ship was enormous, about a city block long. It carried 10,000 pounds of manganese ore and 309 passengers and crew. It reported no problems during its routine radio transmissions on the first half of its trip. Suddenly, there were no more messages. American destroyers searched in vain. No debris, oil slick, or signs of the 309 passengers. Not one piece of debris of a ship as big as a city block.

In the 1950s UFOs researchers circulated a story, very interesting. A witness of a UFO sighting was in a restaurant when he was approached by a very tall man in black—a very weird-looking man who sat next to him—and started talking nonsense and told the wit- ness, "You know, people who look for UFOs find problems." The witness stated that the man in black picked up a quarter, and as the quarter disappeared, disintegrated, he said, "You see how this quarter disappeared? I can make anybody disappear." After six months, the UFO witness died of a heart attack. He was in good health and only thirty-five years old.

Interestingly, some scuba divers have disappeared from clear water not far from their diving boats. For instance, David La France, while checking his boat's bottom with Ann Gunderson and Archie Forfar off Andros Reef, was watched by support divers in their descent of no return. Dr. Morris, his wife, and a guest disappeared while diving from their boat off St. Lucia. Furthermore, people disappeared from beaches and lighthouses. Some ask, how could ships survive and only the people disappear? The fact is that whatever happened to the ship or aircraft happened so suddenly that there was no time to send a call for help or Mayday.

Case (52): Last messages from pilots of ships and planes. Interestingly, pilots of ships and planes, before vanishing, usually have routine communications that give no sign of impending disaster. Sometimes there are messages that expressed surprise, bewilderment, or fear, without indicating the origin or source that confronted them. Also, it seems that the crews of the ships and planes did not perceive or recognize any danger. For instance, the DC-3, a chartered passenger plane approaching Miami for a landing, the pilot announced, "We are approaching the field. We can see the lights of Miami now. Will stand by for landing instructions." After the message, the plane dis- appeared. No debris, oil slick, or bodies were ever found. Similarly, the Star Tiger plane's last official message was, "Weather and performance excellent. Expect to arrive on schedule." Right after that, it vanished. The pilot of Flight #370's last message was "All right, good night" before it went lost and disappeared. Another pilot's last message was "All well" before it vanished.

Moreover, the famous racing yachtsman Harvey Conover sent a cheerful last message from his yacht, the *Renovoc*. Coming through the Florida Keys to his yacht club, he said that he would arrive "for- ty-five minutes. Save a place at the bar." Unfortunately, he never arrived, and neither he nor his boat were ever seen again.

Furthermore, was the case of the *unsinkable* yacht, *Witchcraft*, the owner, Dan Burack, and his passenger, Father Patrick Norgan. The *Witchcraft* was out in buoy No. 7 in the Miami Harbor. They were very close to the shore to admire the Christmas lights in Miami. Suddenly, a call to the Coast Guard for help was made because it seemed that the yacht's propeller had been damaged by something. When the Coast Guard cutter arrived, there was no sign of the *Witchcraft* despite an exhaustive search. However, the final message came after the first call for help. The message was delivered as an aside to Father Norgan while he was still holding the radio key down. He spoke in excitement. The comment was, "I've never seen one like that before." The *Witchcraft* was never found.

Case (53): On April 23, 2007, three brothers disappeared off the Great Barrier Reef in Brisbane, Australia. Authorities believed skipper, Des Batten, fifty-six, and brothers, Peter and James, ages sixty-nine and sixty-three, may have been swept off the *Katz II* sail yacht when they were hit by rough seas. The catamaran was found drifting off Australia's Great Barrier Reef with sails up, engine running, and food on the table. The three brothers were never found. The Coast Guard found an emergency beacon, three life jackets, and a dinghy. The food and cutlery were laid out neatly on the table. Why didn't the rough seas sweep the table with the food and cutlery?

Case (54): In 2009, the publisher and former diplomat Philip Merril, age seventy-two, disappeared, and his sailboat was found sit- ting on the water with its engine running. He was an experienced sailor. According to his family, "He has been an avid yachtsman since he first learned to sail at age seven. He has been actively cruising the Chesapeake Bay since 1958." The Coast Guard sent aircraft and boats with the assumption that Mr. Merril *fell overboard.* The Coast Guard said, "When we found the boat, the engine was running and his wallet was found on board the vessel. No signs of foul play were found." He was never found.

Case (55): The famous nineteenth-century case of the *Mary Celeste.* The *Mary Celeste* was a ship found drifting in mid-ocean. The ship was in perfect condition. The captain and crew had disappeared. No reason for the disappearance has ever been found. The *Mary Celeste* left from New York harbor on November 5, 1872. In addition to the captain, his wife, and an infant daughter, it carried a crew of eight. On December 5 the crew of the ship *Dei Gratia* sighted the *Mary Celeste* drifting, so the captain sent a boarding boat. The ship seemed abandoned. The logbook, which recorded every- thing that happened on the voyage, was found with the captain's papers. All the plates with food were on the table, ready to be eaten. The captain had left all his personal possessions. The sailors had even left their pipes and tobacco. No seaman would forget his pipe. The logbook gave no clue. The captain and his family and the eight crew- men were never found anywhere on earth.

Case (56): Furthermore, in this case, a small fishing boat named *Lady Cecelia* went down in a matter of seconds, seventeen miles off the rugged coast of southern Washington when the Coast Guard reached the scene. According to the Coast Guard, there was nothing but an oil slick, an empty life raft, and some crab pots. The boat was a seventy-foot trawler with the skipper and three crewmen missing. The skipper had practiced the life-and-death task of getting into his survival suit. He perfected the technique so he could do it in thirteen seconds. It seems that whatever took the four men was so fast that they didn't have time to Mayday. The Coast Guard found no survivors in a search area of 640 square miles.

Case (57): In June 1874, the *Iron Mountain* set out from Vicksburg for New Orleans carrying fifty-seven passengers and towing a string of barges. As she reached a bend, the pilot gave a long blast of the steamboat's whistle. The *Iron Mountain* rounded the bend and was never seen again. The barges were later found with the tow ropes cut clean through. Shockingly, there was no wreckage from the big steamer or of the fifty-seven passengers. Hundreds of miles of river bottom were dragged without success. Although there were other boats that should have seen the *Iron Mountain*, shockingly, nobody reported seeing her. The question is, how could the 180-foot vessel and fifty-seven people vanish without a trace on the Mississippi River? Also, except for a few deep sections, the water was nowhere sufficiently deep to cover the *Iron Mountain* completely. Shockingly, no debris or bodies were found.

UFOs or USOs in the oceans and water in the world. Additionally, it is well known to UFO researchers that UFOs have been seen and are called USOs. Undersea crafts were reported in the early beginnings of the UFO wave in the 1940s. USOs have been seen going into and coming out of the water. For instance, in January 1952, a commander of the US Navy reported on a clear day with good weather. Commander Bodler's ship had passed through the Strait of Hormuz bound for India. The third mate called Bodler to the bridge, saying he had spotted something which the commander should see. When he arrived, they saw a luminous band which seemed to be pulsating. The glowing light seemed to be approaching the vessel. The pulsations seemed to start at the center of the band of light. When the lighted area was about a mile from the ship, they could see it was circular in shape, from 1,000 to 1,500 feet in diameter. The pulsations were apparently caused by the revolving motion of an entire light pattern. It was a giant UFO.

Likewise, the waters of South America have been particularly very busy with USO sightings. For example, on December 13, 1959, the Swedish ship *Dorthemaersk* radioed La Guaira, Venezuela, the following message, "We have just seen a strange craft descending from the sky, giving off strange flares. Shaped like a cone, very brilliant." The position given was north of Orchila Island. The crew saw how the object entered the water. After the object submerged, the surface of the sea became brilliant with many colors and very turbulent around it.

Moreover, on April 29, 1961 at about 4:00 p.m., a witness in Newport, Rhode Island, a contractor, was working on a home close to the beach, when his attention was directed to a red sphere bobbing on the waves. So he went one floor up in the house to see better. The witness saw the object rise from the surface of the water to a height of about sixty feet, then move out to sea at an amazing speed. The UFO disappeared.

In another incident on July 28, 1962 that a fishing boat reported, the skipper's account was that he saw a light low in the water and apparently stationary. The skipper used his binoculars and saw a squat, lighted structure in which several men were working. "It appeared to be the stern of a submarine. We could see five men— two in all-white garb, two in dark trousers and white shirts, and one in a sky blue jumpsuit. We passed a beam at about a quarter mile, and I was certain it was a submarine low in the water, steel gray, no markings, decks almost awash, with only its tail and an odd structure showing," the skipper and crew reported. The men further stated, "The object started toward their boat. They had to turn hard to keep clear. It then swept past them at surprising speed and headed toward the open sea." The crew said they heard no noise and saw no trailing from the object.

Also, in June 1959, the Argentinian Navy reported a fast object like a submarine. The object was shaped like a huge fish. The object was extremely fast. Moreover, an unidentified undersea object was responsible for the sinking of the yacht, *Hattie D*, on Wednesday, February 5, 1964. The *Hattie D* was a converted Navy search and rescue ship. The ship was struck off the coast of Cape Mendocino, California. The captain and crew were rescued and reported, "I don't care how deep it was. What holed us was steel, and a long piece. There was no give to it at all." All eleven survivors, including the cap- tain and his wife, insisted that the yacht had struck or been rammed by a *metal object*.

Similarly, on the night of September 12, 1963, nineteen men of the ship *Texas Tower II* off Cape Cod reported to the Coast Guard by radio that they had spotted an object. The crew asked for an investigation, and a Coast Guard boat was dispatched to investigate. The crew stated that the object was a UFO, had a light, and that smoke and steam had appeared on the surface.

Moreover, on October 31, 1963, several people near Iguapos, Brazil, watched a twenty-five-foot-diameter silver disc which flew over the area. The object dived into the river and the water began to boil and an eruption of mud followed. The witnesses made great efforts to save the UFO but they were unsuccessful. The Peropava is a river twelve feet deep at the point where the disc sank, and the bot- tom is composed of about fifteen feet of mud and clay. The authorities believed that if the UFO sank to the bottom, as the rising mud seemed to indicate, the UFO went right through the mud to the solid rock beneath. The UFO simply disappeared.

On March 16, 1966 in Brazil, a white ovoid object plunged into the Atlantic Ocean, close to Cagarras Island. Many people watched the object fall and plunge into the sea. Similarly, in Venezuela in August 1967, many witnesses reported UFOs going into or coming out of the sea. On the fourth of August, 1967, Hugo Sierra Yepes, an engineer, was on the beach about sixteen miles north of Recife. It was early morning and the visibility was excellent. He was suddenly startled to see a UFO, which appeared to be two concavities joined by a ring, coming out of the water some distance from the shore. The ring, which seemed to join the two parts, had triangles of blue and red on it, but the main body was gray, apparently metallic. It then rose slowly toward the east, and finally picked up tremendous speed and disappeared into the sky. Yepes estimated that the whole incident took no more than one minute.

In another incident in Salina, Venezuela, a witness reported a disc-shaped object and giving off a very bright orange glow. The disc rose out of the sea at about 500 meters from shore, hovered for a few seconds, then rose obliquely into the sky, disappearing within seconds. Another witness was in the area of Salina, six miles off the resort city of Arrecifes. The witness was shocked that the sea started to *wrinkle up* in a vast round area. Soon the water began to turn a lighter hue, then a light blue shade, and finally a brilliant orange shade. The witness noticed a *deafening* sound. He also felt a tingling sensation in his feet. At this point, a huge *pancake-shaped* object emerged from the sea, hovering, and left toward Maiquetia in a slanting ascending pattern.

The next similar incident was a daytime sighting. A witness was on a rock on the beach at Catia la Mar, looking out to sea, then he saw a disturbance in the water, as if the ocean was *boiling*, and thought he was about to see a submarine. Shockingly, one after another, three disc-shaped gray objects emerged from the water and flew off out to sea.

Many UFO researchers hypothesized that undersea UFOs or USOs might be based on the ocean floor. Obviously, such bases would afford first-class concealment. Scientists know that the seabed is full of mountains as high as 40,000 feet. Also in the oceans are canyons. UFOs are capable of traveling through space; certainly, they are able to navigate in the water. It is possible that the intelligence behind the UFO phenomena have an interest in mining. However, a technological alien civilization that can teleport planes, ships, and people can create anything from nothing because they can manipulate matter at the quantum level.

On October 24, 1980, the US freighter named *Post* bound for Egypt with a cargo of yellow corn and a crew of thirty-four suddenly disappeared without even sending a distress or Mayday call. It was never found nor the crew. The Coast Guard conducted a ten-day air search covering 300,000 square miles. A 12,000-ton freighter disappeared; they reported no problems. No wreckage, oil slick, or bodies were found.

CHAPTER III

UFOs and Cases
of Teleportation on Land

"Living is easy with eyes closed, misunderstanding all you see."
—The Beatles, "Strawberry Fields Forever" (1967)

As I have shown in the two previous chapters, teleportation also takes place on land.

Case (58): In 1924, two experienced RAF pilots crash-landed in the Iraqi desert during a routine short flight. When they failed to arrive, rescue parties were sent out to look for them and the plane. The rescue party found the plane but not the pilots. The search team only found footsteps leading away from it, showing that the two men had set off on foot in the direction of their destination, but after a short distance, the footsteps stopped. Interestingly, there were no signs of a skirmish and no other footprints in the sand. The men's tracks just stopped suddenly—one foot in front of the other, indicating that they had been walking normally when something happened that the two men vanished and were never seen again.

Case (59): In another case in 1900, three fishermen went to relieve three lighthouse keepers. They found nothing wrong at the lighthouse. There were no hints of damage or accident, no disorder, no signs of panic, no missing boats, no messages—and no men. The three keepers had simply vanished off the face of the earth.

Case (60): In 1909, Oliver Thomas, an eleven-year-old boy, walked out of a Christmas Eve party outside the house. Suddenly, the guests in the party heard a cry that seemed to come from above the house, but they saw nothing. The guests looked all over, but the boy was never found.

Case (61): During the Spanish War of Succession, 4,000 troops disappeared on a march through the Pyrenees.

Case (62): In 1858, 650 French colonial troops marching toward Saigon vanished fifteen miles from the city.

Case (63): In 1939, 2,988 Chinese troops stationed south of Nanking vanished, leaving their camp in perfect order, their rifles neatly stacked.

Case (64): During World War II, a US Navy blimp patrolling the San Francisco harbor was seen suddenly to soar up into a cloud, only to reappear minutes later without the two crewmen.

Case (65): On November 12, 1975, Middie Rivers, a seventy- five-year-old hunting guide, was leading a group of hikers. He was pacing just in front of the group when he suddenly disappeared without a trace. He was never found, despite the fact that the police, as well as hundreds of volunteers, looked for him.

Case (66): In 1854, a slave owner named Williansson vanished while crossing a field near Selma, Alabama, in sight of his family and neighbors.

Case (67): Similarly, in 1977, a teenage girl vanished in the same area in which Rivers disappeared. She had gone on a hike. She was seen by several people at different points in her walk, until she simply vanished. Volunteers, police, and dogs searched every- where around the area where she was last seen, but she never was found.

Case (68): Likewise, James Tetford went to visit a friend to Bennigton, Vermont, which is near Mount Glastonbury. He decided to take the bus and he was seen boarding the bus by several witnesses. A thorough investigation could reveal absolutely no clues to Tetford's strange disappearance. Shockingly, several people saw him board the bus but no one saw him getting off the bus. Obviously, it would seem impossible to vacate a bus en route to the next station, either voluntarily or involuntarily, without being seen by other passengers and the bus driver. He simply disappeared.

Case (69): Moreover, in August 1970, a woman name Danya went out to a party 150 feet from her house. She left the party at 12:15 a.m. and walked back to her house. Her friends saw her walking back, but she never arrived. She simply vanished.

Case (70): Furthermore, in Indiana in 1889 Oliver Larch, and David Lang in Tennessee in 1880. In both cases, the victims walked out of their homes and just vanished seconds later. Shockingly, their voices were heard calling for help, but their bodies were nowhere to be found. They simply disappeared; teleported somewhere.

Case (71): By the same token, on July 13, 2008 in Holmdel, New Jersey, a retired career military man was last seen by his wife around the backyard of their home. After she reported him missing, the police, volunteers, and emergency personnel looked where the couple lived, but all to no avail. Since his disappearance, the family has listed his name with national and state missing people's registries. Also, his name was featured on the *America's Most Wanted* website. For the family, it is a mystery because he left his car keys, his checkbook, and the medicine he takes for several health conditions. Also, he left his cigarettes which, being a chain-smoker, is baffling. The cigarettes were on the table. The couple had an active life together and had plans to meet friends for bingo. She said, "You don't just disappear off the face of the earth without something." As I write this book on February 27, 2017, he has never been found.

Case (72): Similarly, a New Jersey woman seeks her brother who disappeared. She stated to the police, "He was outside his house, sitting in his car, and then he was gone." She is asking for help in trying to find her fifty-four-year-old brother. She added, "The car was still there." Her brother limps, walks with a cane or walker, and has been unemployed with a disability for at least five years. He dis- appeared without his eyeglasses or his medications. Also, she said that he was *bummed out* after being diagnosed with diabetes a month earlier. Furthermore, three dozen rescuers with dogs searched the sur- rounding woods and the nearby creeks for two days. The search was called off because the dogs could not pick up her brother's scent. He simply vanished. Also, there has been no activity in his bank account or credit card. She said, "I've contacted anyone I can think of and no one has heard from him." He simply vanished.

Case (73): On November 29, 1809, Benjamin Bathurst, an employee of the British Foreign Office, was to board a coach outside an inn near Berlin. He went to look at the horses and vanished for- ever. He simply disappeared.

Case (74): In June 1900, Sherman Church ran into a cotton mill at August Mills near Lake Michigan. He never came out and could not be found.

Case (75): In 1974, pigs, sheep, and heifers vanished from two farms near Manchester, England.

Case (76): In 2009, Mrs. Bishop went for a walk and never came back. On a warm summer evening, she gave her husband of fifty years a kiss, told him she loved him, and then she left their summer home in South Seaside Park, New Jersey, to take a stroll on the beach. She hasn't been seen since. She was a seventy-two-year-old grand- mother. She walked off into the sunshine, never to be seen or heard from again. A big search and rescue was organized with hundreds of volunteers. They walked the beach. Also, they went door to door asking for her. They combed through the vegetation in the wilderness of Island Beach State Park. Unfortunately, even with the assistance of tracking dogs, helicopters, boats, and drones, there was no trace of the lady. A relative said, "I don't know how someone can disappear off the face of the earth without somebody seeing something." The search team checked backyards, garages, outdoor showers, motels, and sex offenders. Also, the state police combed the beach on horse- back. Her husband said, "She kissed me. We said 'I love you' like we always did, and then she took a walk." The couple had a very solid marriage, with family and friends. She simply vanished forever.

Case (77): In 1914 during the First World War, the British Norfolk regiment of more than 250 soldiers marched into a mysterious cloud and forever disappeared. UFOs appear in the form of clouds.

Case (78): A retired military man served his country in Vietnam. In 2007, he vanished. There was no note, no signs of suicide, homicide, or foul play. Seven years after his disappearance, his family continued to look for answers. He had chronic obstructive pulmonary disease for which he needed an inhaler. He left his car keys, credit cards, the inhaler and medication, his cigarettes, and his veteran's identification cards. He didn't own a cellular phone. His family, volunteers, firefighters, and dogs searched woods and areas surrounding his home. However, they found no clues as to where he may have gone. Also, they didn't find anything in the national database on missing persons. Furthermore, the family and volunteers checked hospitals in New Jersey and homeless shelters. The family checked the tent city in Lakewood and taxi and bus companies. Furthermore, detectives stated, since his disappearance, no one has used or applied for a credit card in his name. He simply vanished.

Case (79): The most baffling and shocking mystery was the disappearance of Graham Marsden in England. In January one day at 5:00 a.m., he filled up his car with gas. After paying his bill, he asked for the bathroom. Witnesses saw him walking toward it. After an hour, the gas station attendant went to look for the man, finding no trace of him. He called the police who searched the surrounding woods with tracker dogs. However, there was no signs of the man. The police stated, "If he planned to disappear, why would he fill his car with petrol first and leave it at the pump? And why choose a service station mile from anywhere? We are just mystified."

Case (80): The village that vanished. The Canadian police are still trying to solve the mystery of why an entire village of 1,200 people and even the dead from their graves vanished without a trace. The mystery began in 1930 when trapper Armand Laurent and his two sons saw a strange gleam crossing Canada's northern sky. Laurent said, "The huge light changed shape from moment to moment so that it was now cylindrical, now like an enormous bullet." A few days later, a couple of Mounties stopped at Laurent's cabin to seek shelter on their way to Lake Anjikuni where one of them explained there was a kind of problem. The Mountie asked a puzzled Laurent if the light he had sighted had been heading toward the lake. Laurent answered it had. The Mountie nodded without further comment. The Royal Canadian Mounted Police were already busy with the strangest case in their history. Furthermore, another trapper named Joe Labelle walked around the village and had "been oppressed by an odd sense of dread. Normally, it was a noisy settlement of 1,200 people." The village was locked in silence, and no smoke drifted from a single chimney. The boats and kayaks were still tied up at the shore. When he went from door to door, he found the men's rifles. No Eskimo traveler would leave his rifle at home. Likewise, inside the huts, pots of caribou stew had grown moldy. Also, a parka lay on a bunk with two bone needles beside it. However, Labelle found no bodies, living or dead, and no sign of violence. At some point in a normal day, close to mealtime, it appeared there had been a sudden interruption in daily life. Furthermore, Joe Labelle contacted the Royal Canadian Police. After a few hours, they found the sled dogs tied to the trees near the village. Shockingly, the burial grounds were open graves from which, in subzero temperatures, the bodies of the dead had been removed, although there was no possible means of transportation by which the people could have fled. The police were unable to believe that 1,200 people could vanish off the face of the earth. No footprints in the snow were found. The police searched all of Canada. The search continued for years. After half a century, the case remains unsolved. The village simply vanished.

Case (81): The disappearance of the Roanoke Island settlers. According to history books, it took three years for Governor John White to return from England with supplies to the settlers in Roanoke Island. White and over one hundred colonists had settled on the island off the American coast in 1587. Ultimately, when supplies ran low, the governor headed back to England to replenish them. In his return trip to Roanoke Island, all kinds of bad fortune confronted him, from bad weather, pirate attacks, and the war between England and Spain. Furthermore, when White finally reached Roanoke Island, he was shocked to discover that his friends and family were gone. A desperate search began, but no trace of the settlers was ever found. Interestingly, over three centuries, many historians have made many guesses. Among the questions—were the settlers killed by Indians? Did they move to a safer place? Did they intermarry with the Indians? Why is there no evidence of their living or dying? Were they teleported like in Case 79, the village that vanished?

Case (82): What happened to the Clovis, the first and lost Americans? The absence of Clovis and Folsom man from the fossil record is outstanding. Certainly, no camping site of prehistoric times around the world is devoid of human bones. If they didn't actually bury their dead, caves are found with animal remains. Even if the Clovis were too primitive to bury their dead, we should be able to find remains of these hunters. All the archeological research doesn't reveal a house or even a crude wooden structure. Even a skin tent would reveal who the Clovis were. Are we to suppose that Clovis and Folsom man didn't wrap himself in a bison skin and weather out the wet and glacial days and nights? The glacial winds coming from the ice masses to the north were extremely cold. The Clovis hunters lived 11,000 years ago.

Case (83): The mystery of the Mayans. Some historians believed that the Mayans abandoned their cities; that their cities were empty. The Mayans were very advanced in astronomy and mathematics. Their sophistication is beyond belief. Not even the Europeans were so advanced. The Mayans survived in the jungles of Central America. There was no reason to abandon their cities. Or probably something like Case 79, the village that disappeared, took place?

Case (84): In this case, on January 4, 1975, waiter Carlos Diaz was walking home from work in Bahia Blanca, Argentina, early in the morning. Suddenly, he was blinded by a pulsating light and heard a whine like a radio wave. He said later that the air and even the street seemed to vibrate. Then he felt himself being lifted off his feet and carried into the air. When he was ten feet up, he looked down and passed out. He woke in what seemed to be a bright flowing sphere. As if in a dream, he saw three silent, green-skinned creatures standing nearby. They plucked tufts of hair from his head and it did not hurt. Four hours after he was whisked from the streets of Bahia Blanca, Diaz was found lying beside a road in Buenos Aires, 500 miles away. Close to him was a bag containing his work clothes. He rushed to a nearby hospital, and doctors found him to be in good health but shocked. They could not understand how hair had been tugged out of his head without damaging the roots.

Case (85): In 1968, Dr. Geraldo Vidal and his wife were driving near Bahia Blanca when they saw something like a cloud envelop their car. Time seemed to stand still. Suddenly, they were driving but the road and scenery had changed. They stopped to check and eventually found they were in Mexico. The couple could not account for being 3,000 miles from Argentina. They had no recollection of bright lights; no feeling of being lifted into the air. The car was taken to the mechanics and they found strange scorch marks on the bodywork of their car.

Case (86): In another case, Jose Antonio Da Silva remembered what happened to him after he vanished from Vitoria, Brazil, on May 9, 1969. He was found wandering around, trancelike, in Bebedouro, 500 miles away, four days later. He said creatures about four feet tall had plucked him from the ground and carried him off to another planet. Incredulous Brazilians had to admit that something odd had happened to him. He was clearly frightened, constantly darting his eyes skywards, and terrified of bright lights.

Case (87): Furthermore, in another case, a soldier was found stumbling in bewilderment around Mexico City's main square in 1593. He was dressed with a uniform and weapons of a regiment more than 9,000 miles away. Questioned by the Inquisition, he answered he had no idea how he had gotten to Mexico. He had no sensation of traveling. His last recollection was of standing outside the presidential palace of Manila in the Philippines on guard.

Case (88): In another case, the Inquisition was also called to investigate when a man appeared mysteriously in Portugal in 1655 and claimed that just seconds earlier he had been outside his house in India. His last memory was of finding himself whisked into the air. The Inquisition decided he had occult powers or that the devil had contact with him and burned him at the stake.

Case (89): The magician's close call to be teleported. The most shocking experience was that of the stage magician William Neff. This amazing event took place at the Paramount Theatre in New York. There were a few witnesses to the event. The witnesses were trans- fixed by the gradual dematerialization of the magician. He became so translucent that the stage curtains could be seen through him. Curiously, the magician seemed to be unaware of his weird state and continued with his performance. Gradually, he became solid again, slowly materializing. He was asked about the dematerialization. He answered that he didn't know why it was happening, although he said that on two occasions he partially dematerialized. He didn't know why or who caused this phenomenon.

Case (90): Romulus and Remus, founders of Rome. The first ruler of Rome was Romulus. He ruled Rome for thirty-seven years where- upon he disappeared. The Roman myth mentions that he was taken up into the sky by a whirlwind.

Case (91): The story in the Bible said that Elijah and Elisha were walking, conversing, when suddenly "a chariot of fire and horses of fire separated the two of them, and Elijah went up by a whirlwind into heaven." And Elisha saw it and cried, "My father, my father, the chariots of Israel and its horsemen." Only the mantle of Elijah was left behind, and Elisha took it up.

Case (92): In 96 AD, Apollonius of Tyana, a philosopher and first-century teacher who was known throughout the Roman Empire, vanished mysteriously while walking down the road at age 100.

Case (93): Legion IX Hispana (Ninth Spanish Legion) was a Roman legion with cavalry from 3,000 to 6,000 men stationed in Britain during the Roman conquest of Britain in 108–164 AD. The legion disappeared from historical records without explanation in the second century. There are many hypotheses regarding their fate and why there is no record of their fate. Probably like in Case 79, the village that disappeared, the same thing happened to the Spanish legion.

Case (94): In 1812, Theodiosia Burr Alston (twenty-nine), daughter of US Vice President Aaron Burr, sailed from Georgetown, South Carolina, aboard the *Patriot*, and she was never seen again.

Case (95): In 1829, John Lansing Jr. (seventy-five), an American politician, left his Manhattan hotel to mail a letter at a New York City dock and was never seen again.

Case (96): In 1848, Khachatur Abovian (thirty-eight), a famous nineteenth-century writer, left his house early one morning and was never heard from again.

CHAPTER IV
UFOs and Teleportation

"An intelligence knowing at a given instance of time, all forces acting in nature, as well as the momentary position of all things of which the Universe consists would be able to comprehend the motions of the largest bodies of the world and those of the lightest atoms in one single formula, provided his intellect were sufficiently powerful to subject all data to analysis; to him nothing would be uncertain but past and future would be present in his eyes."

—Pierre Simon Laplace (1749–1827)

Teleportation is not a concept borrowed from voodoo religion, black magic, witchcraft, or the occult. Teleportation is a scientific concept which is the theoretical transportation of matter through space and time by converting it into energy and then reconverting it at the terminal point. Also, there is a popular phenomenon named poltergeist which is caused by the same principles and intelligence behind the UFO phenomenon. In fact, teleportation is no longer the stuff of science fiction. *Star Trek* was the first television show that gave us a view of what teleportation is, although the current development of science only allowed the teleportation of subatomic particles. Probably, it will take the human race a couple of hundred years to be able to teleport people, planes, and ships. Scientists, from Einstein to Hawkins, know the basis of teleportation. The physical basis for teleportation is the baffling phenomenon of entanglement. This is a bizarre shifting between nature's tiniest particles, no matter how far apart they are. Furthermore, in 1997 in a small laboratory at the University of Innsbruck, scientists teleported a few quanta of light in one way.

By the same token, in 2001, an amazing story appeared on the Internet. "The Department of Defense announced that research scientists at the Massachusetts Institute of Technology have successfully tested the first quantum teleportation. Two white mice, weighing 87 and 90 grams each, received clear bills of health after they were simultaneously converted to photons of light and then transported 13.7 meters through a hydrogen gas tube. They were interstitially reconstituted within 10 seconds and exhibited physical movements 17 seconds later." Surprisingly, if it is true, this amazing technological advance was never announced to the world.

Likewise, scientist Anton Zeilinger, in a 2000 scientific article, wrote, "The entanglement of molecules and then their teleportation may reasonably be expected within the next decade; what happens beyond is anybody's guess." On the other hand, another scientist, Hans Christian, stated, "But it would take an unbelievable amount of data processing. Even a coffee cup without the coffee would take many times the age of the Universe." In other words, we would need a computer more super powerful than any we have on earth right now. A very advanced quantum computer will enable simulations of physical process at the quantum level. The everyday experience tells us that the only way to affect or move an object is in direct contact— you move the object or send a signal.

As a matter of fact, information or energy must travel through space and time in order to affect an object. However, Albert Einstein postulated in his special theory of relativity that nothing can travel faster than the speed of light of 186,000 kilo- meters per second. Interestingly, the laws of relativity do not apply in the process of teleportation. The reason is that at the quantum level physical processes are instantaneous. The theory of relativity applies only to the macroworld—galaxies, planets, stars, and the universe. The laws of entanglement are nonlocal. For instance, a measurement of particle A affects its entangled partner B instantaneously, whatever the separation distance and without any signal or influence passing between the two locations. For example, the photons of light coming from Andromeda Galaxy take two million years to arrive to Earth, so the light we are receiving right now left the Andromeda galaxy when Australopithecus was walking the savannahs of Africa.

On the other hand, if, for example, an alien civilization wants to teleport a plane from Earth to Andromeda Galaxy, it will be instantaneous. The entanglement affects whatever the separation distance. The quantum connection is not affected by fields of force, gravity, electromagnetism, time, or space. In addition, it doesn't weaken as the particles move apart because it doesn't stretch across space. Indeed, in entanglement, it's as if the particles were right next to one another. In fact, the effect and force is as powerful at a million light years as it is a millimeter away.

More shockingly, teleportation operates outside time and space. In entanglement, what happens at A is immediately known at B. Interestingly, Einstein's opinion was that entanglement was *spooky* and *telepathic*. Also, he said that "the tie that binds entangled particles is a physical absurdity." For Einstein, the idea that an effect could go faster-than-light speeds and connect causally isolated objects was to Einstein a scientific and intellectual outrage. In addition, according to scientists, the phenomenon of entanglement does not violate causality because no information passes between the entangled particles. More shocking, the information is already built into the combined system of particles and no measurement can add to it. For Einstein, it was very hard to accept quantum physics because the ghostly long- range behavior means that quantum mechanics as it is *couldn't be the final word*. It was *a mere approximation of some as yet undiscovered description of nature.*

One of the most bizarre and astonishing revelations of quantum physics is that the entire universe is intimately connected at the quantum level. Furthermore, at the beginning of the universe in the *Big Bang* fourteen to twenty billion years ago, all matter, time, space, and energy were huddled together inside a ball much smaller than a period or a comma. However, in entanglement, the interactions between particles given that the universe is expanding, the particles are connected. Conversely, if you make the slightest change at the quantum level, it will have some effect instantaneously throughout all known physical reality.

Moreover, in the late 1980s, physicist theoreticians began to see entanglement not just as a puzzle but as a way to discover the mystery of the quantum world, and also as a new form of communication and computing. So the link between quantum mechanics and the information theory evolved as the quantum information science. The most stunning aspect of this field is teleportation. As a matter of fact, a new theory of the universe stated that the basic nature of everything around us isn't matter but information.

Likewise, the scientist Thomas Durt of Vrije University in Brussels believes that entanglement is ubiquitous with the similar equations that led Schrödinger to discover entanglement. Shockingly, Durt made the astonishing discovery that almost all quantum inter- actions result in entanglement, whatever the conditions. He stated, "When you see light coming from a faraway star, the photon is almost certainly entangled with atoms of the star and the atoms encountered along the way. The continuous interactions between electrons in the atoms of all objects and substances ensure that everything is a spaghetti-like mass of entanglements, and we humans are no exception." Indeed, not even the theory of relativity stands in the way because the speed of light does not apply in the microscopic world, only in the macro universe. Nonetheless, to make teleportation of a human a reality, scientists have to discover the way to duplicate the quantum states of all the particles in a human body. They will need super- computers and devices probably based on nanotechnology that can deconstruct and reconstruct a system of trillions of particles in perfect order at astonishing speed. Additionally, Hans Christian, a physicist, stated, "In principle, you can recreate anything anywhere, just as long as you send information on the object luminaly. You have the raw materials and you're willing to destroy the original. But it would take an unbelievable amount of data processing." In fact, we would need a supercomputer more powerful than anything we have ever seen on this earth. It has to be a super powerful quantum computer.

Nevertheless, the use of the term *teleport* to describe the hypothetical movement of material objects between one place and another without physically traversing the distance between them has been known since 1878. The American writer Charles Fort is credited with having coined the word *teleportation* in 1931 to describe the strange disappearances and appearances of objects which he suggested may be connected.

Furthermore, in his book *The Physics of Star Trek*, writer Lawrence M. Krauss mentions that there are two essential stages of the process of teleportation—dematerialization and re-materialization. In order to dematerialize something, the binding energy of electrons, atoms, and all its nuclei would have to be overcome. He notes that the binding energy of electrons around nuclei is minor relative to binding energy that holds nuclei together. He states, "If we were to heat up the nuclei to about 1,000 billion degrees (about a mil- lion times hotter than the temperature at the core of the sun), then not only would the quarks inside lose their binding energies, but at around this temperature matter will suddenly lose all of its mass." So matter will turn into radiation; matter will dematerialize. In energy units, this implies providing about 10 percent of the rest mass of pro- tons and neutrons in the form of heat. Actually, to heat up a body the size of a human being to this level would require about 10 percent of the energy needed to annihilate the material or the energy equivalent of a *hundred 1-megaton hydrogen bombs!*

So how much energy would be required to teleport a plane of the size of Malaysian Airlines Flight #370? For the intelligence behind the UFO phenomenon with this technology, the possibilities are infinite. Can they teleport asteroids like the one that caused the mass extinction of the dinosaurs to help evolution with the creation of Homo sapiens? Do they move the moon close to us to help us to dream? At the quantum level, they can create life and even worlds, just like gods. However, it seems out of reach for humankind to tele- port people and objects.

In this event, I will show how easy and neat it is to teleport for the intelligence behind the UFO phenomenon. In the autumn of 1977 in England and around the world, there was a wave of UFO sightings. At a farm not too far from London, the Coombs family reported to law enforcement a UFO sighting. The first major event occurred on April 16. Mrs. Coombs was driving home late at night with three of her children. Suddenly, her ten-year-old son Keiron, who was in the back seat, reported a strange light in the sky. The light was the size of a basketball, yellowish with a harsh grayish light underneath and a torch-like beam shining down from it. Keiron told his mother that the light had U-turned and was following them. The UFO caught up with the car and traveled along beside it, at which point the car lights began to fade. The light moved to the side and kept watching the family until they arrived home.

Likewise, on April 22, Mr. and Mrs. Coombs were watching a late night movie. At about 11:30 p.m., they became aware of a glow outside their window. The UFO was quietly watching the family. The following day the family reported a case of teleportation. "Sometimes one or two cows disappeared, but frequently the entire herd had disappeared from the farm." Shockingly, the family received angry calls from their neighboring farmer, asking him to come to collect his herd of thirty cows. Mrs. Coombs insisted that the animals had been properly fastened in their farm. All the doors had been secured, insisting that they had secured the bolt with binder twine as an extra precaution. The family stated, "To escape in the way indicated, the herd would have had to move past the cottage." Yet neither he nor she nor the rest of the family had seen the thirty cows pass the cottage or heard a sound. Mr. Coombs said, "There simply had not been enough time between the moment at which the cattle were last seen and the moment when they were reported at the other farm for them to have *traversed* the distance in any natural way!" The shocking implication is that thirty cows were teleported without causing any noise, and the family didn't see or hear anything unusual. After the family recovered their cattle, the cattle were very frightened and the milk yield was down.

Similarly, in another farm not too far from Mr. and Mrs. Coombs, the owner reported that cows and horses were found in different places. For instance, a cow and a horse were found up in the hayloft. How did they get there? Nobody in the farm would move them up in the hayloft.

In this example, we see how easy it is for the intelligence behind the UFO phenomenon to teleport.

Actually, the UFO doesn't have to be present for a person or object to be teleported. It seems to me that they have a view of the planet. That is the reason they teleport people and planes anywhere in the world. Furthermore, a paper published in *Nature Photonics* and coauthored by engineers at NASA's Jet Propulsion Laboratory in Pasadena, California, reported experiments with quantum teleportation in a metropolitan fiber cable network. According to this article, for first time teleportation occurred over long distances in a city infra- structure. Moreover, in Canada at the University of Calgary, researchers teleported the quantum state of a photon more than 3.7 miles (6 kilometers) in *dark* (unused) cables under the city of Calgary. That's a *new record* for the *longest distance* of *quantum teleportation* in a metropolitan network. Actually, longer distances had been recorded in the past, although these experiments were conducted in lab settings where photons were fired through spools of cable to simulate the loss of signal caused by long distances. However, this latest experiment in Calgary tested quantum teleportation in an infrastructure which is a major step forward for the technology.

As a matter of fact, Francesco Marsili said, "Demonstrating quantum effects such as teleportation outside of a lab environment involves a new set of challenges. This experiment shows how these challenges can all be overcome and hence it marks an import- ant milestone towards the future quantum Internet." Also, he said, "Quantum communication unlocks some of the unique properties of quantum mechanics to, for example, exchange information with ultimate security or link together quantum computers."

Likewise, scientists said, "The superconducting detector plat- form which has been pioneered by JPL and NIST researchers makes it possible to detect single photons at telecommunications wavelengths with nearly perfect efficiency and almost no noise. This was simply not possible with earlier detectors types, and so experiments such as ours, using existing fiber infrastructure, would have been close to impossible." By the same token, scientists who understand the rules of *entanglement* can entangle two particles so that their properties are linked. Entanglement happens with particles with different characteristics or states that can be bound together across space. That means whatever affects one particle's state will affect the other, even if they're located miles apart from one another. For instance, photon 1 and photon 2, and photon 2 is sent to a distant location. There it meets photon 3, and the two interact with each other. Photons 3's state can be transferred to photon 2 and automatically *teleported* to the entangled twin, photon 1. Shockingly, the transfer happens despite the fact that photons 1 and 3 never interact.

Obviously, it will take science a long time before we can teleport a plane as big as Flight #370.

CHAPTER V

The Boeing 777 Flight #370 Advanced Technological Features

"On Flight #370, there were multiple transponders and three flight management computers. A failure of one computer or system would result in automatic transfer to another. For air traffic control to lose secondary radar contact, someone would have to deactivate all three systems. And even then, there would still be primary (military) radar coverage by Malaysia, India, Indonesia, and Thailand."

—George Hatcher Sr.,
President, Air Crash Consultants

"(Airplanes) must come down eventually. They can land safely or they may crash. But airplanes don't just disappear. Someone is hiding something."

—Dr. Mahathir Mohamad,
Former Prime Minister of Malaysia

"The Vienna-based Comprehensive Nuclear-Test-Ban Treaty Organization confirmed that neither an explosion nor a plane crash on land or on water had been detected."

—Stephane Dujarric,
Spokesperson for United Nations General Ban Ki-Moon

T

he specifics of the Boeing 777-200ER. The (ER) stands for extended range. This plane was the first aircraft in aviation history to earn FAA (Federal Aviation Administration) approval to fly extended range twin-engine operations since it went into service in 1995. The Boeing 777 can cruise at altitudes up 43,100 feet and has become the flagship of many airlines due to its excellent track record. The Boeing 777 has flown almost five million mile-flights and also is regarded all over the world as an excellent aircraft with the latest technologies commercially available. In addition, the Boeing 777 has a system called *the fly-by-wire* system for primarily flight controls. This is a new automated system that was once only used by advanced military jets. This is a state-of-the-art and precise method in which multiple computer systems of the aircraft actually control the actions of the plane.

Emergency equipment on the Boeing 777-200ER communications systems. There are many methods of communication between the airplane, its pilots, its manufacturer, air traffic control (ATC), satellite functions, normal radar, and military radar. The methods are independent of each other so that if one fails, there are always other options for communication from the plane to ground personnel and for their tracking of the aircraft.

Primary radio contact is via normal radio communications between the flight deck and air traffic control. It is VHF (very high frequency) and HF (high frequency). Furthermore, if ATC suspects that the flight crew is unable to respond via radio frequency, ATC will instruct them to *squawk their ident.* That's accomplished by the simple push of a button in the cockpit that lights up a signal for the controllers at ATC. Squawking the ident of the plane is such a basic emergency communications procedure that all flight crews know how to do it.

Satellite communication systems (Satcom) state of the art technological equipment on the Selective Calling (Selcal) is another tool the aircraft communicates via a unique (or virtually unique) code for each flight. In contrast to what is known, commercials flights are tracked over the ocean. Air crews should always be in contact with both air traffic control and company dispatchers on the ground. Most intercontinental aircrafts even have data link or satellite communications systems that allow for constant real-time tracking. The veteran commercial pilot Patrick Smith gives us a description of how an intercontinental plane is tracked over the oceans. "To be clear, planes are tracked over the ocean, even in remote, non-radar areas. People believed that once a plane hits oceanic airspace, the plane dis- appears until making landfall on the other side. This is not the case at all." Crews are always in touch with both air traffic control and company personnel on the ground, and both of these entities are following and tracking the plane. Transponders aren't used in non-radar areas, but you've also got HF radio Satcom, CPDLC (controller-pilot data link communications), FMC (flight management computer), Datalink, and so forth. Which equipment you're using to communicate depends where you are and which air traffic control facility you are working with.

The transponder. The transponder is a small box that, at regular intervals, emits an electrical signal. *It squawks,* sending a burst of data that reveals information about the plane and its location. A former FAA safety inspector said about Flight #370, "Making it invisible could be accomplished by something as simple as the pilot turning off the transponder. Everything on Flight #370 is triple redundant. The electrical systems, the charging systems, the battery systems, the communications systems, even the transponders are on completely separate busses. The chance that all the electrical systems were out of that aircraft would have indicated a much more massive failure of some kind. Although various news media reported that the transponder of Flight #370 was turned off, that simply has not been proven. We don't have a way of knowing if the transponder was actually turned off. We only know that it stopped working in the manner in which it was designed to work. That could have resulted from an immediate physical catastrophe, like a missile hit, massive fire, or because it was turned off manually. We simply don't know."

Furthermore, an expert in aviation disasters said, "With respect to the missing Malaysian Airlines plane, a discussion of transponders is only partly relevant in the first place. For air traffic control purposes transponders only work in areas of ATC radar coverage. Once beyond a certain distance from the coast, the oceans are not monitored by radar and transponders are not used for tracking. We keep the units turned on because the TCAS anti-collision system is transponder-based, but we rely on Satcom, ACARS (aircraft communications and reporting system), FMS datalink, and other means for position reports and communications. Thus, transponders are pertinent to this story only when the missing plane was close to *land*. Once over the open water, on or off, it didn't matter anyway." A transponder can be turned off. Reports of that are usually referring to what is known as ACARS being turned off, but ACARS is one of the available methods of communication with an aircraft. Another system is called the automatic dependent surveillance manager (ADS) which also automatically sends position reports of the aircraft. Its reports go to both air traffic control and the manufacturer, Boeing in the case of Flight #370. Like ACARS, the ADS system can be turned off manually, but it, too, continues to communicate via satellite when turned off.

Now note that all the following safety and emergency locator systems cannot be turned off. They function automatically and independently of each other. No one has to enable anything in order to make that happen because aircraft communications systems automatically use satellites. Further, there are three emergency locator transmitters on the Boeing 777. One is mounted on top of the air- craft above the passenger cabin and the other two are located on the large exit doors. The ELTs are *armed*, meaning that they are automatically *activated* by extreme circumstances, such as high deceleration forces like a crash or even safe but hard landing. The ELTs can also be activated manually by the flight crew in the event that help is needed. The crew would simply flick a switch in the cockpit and an emergency alarm would immediately flash to ground control. An ELT device emits a distress signal on three separate megahertz frequencies on the aircraft's band network. It was designed to do this in order to guarantee reception of the distress signal anywhere in the world. None of Flight #370's three ELTs have been recovered and *no automatic emergency distress signals were picked up* from any of the three ELTs known to be on board the aircraft at takeoff.

Black boxes are indestructible information recorders that survive a plane crash. Interestingly, they are not actually black in color. *Black box* is just an engineering term for a system that retains scientific information.

They are actually orange. There are two black boxes in the plane—the cockpit voice recorder (CVR) and the FDR. The CVR records all communications between pilots and ATC, as well as all sounds and conversations that take place in the cockpit of the aircraft. It runs automatically from the moment the plane engines are started. The CVR continues running automatically and does not shut itself off until five minutes after the final engine shutdown. It cannot be manually shut off; it does not even have an off switch. It does have an *erase* button, but the erase button will only function if the aircraft is on the ground with the parking brake set. The CVR records in a two-hour loop. It records over itself at the end of every two hours of recording. That would prove problematic if Flight #370 did fly for an extended period of time on autopilot. The CVR is actu- ally mounted on the tail of the aircraft rather than in the cockpit. The purpose of mounting it on the tail of the aircraft is to minimize any possible damage to it during a crash. Most importantly, the CVR has an emergency transmitter that is automatically activated by impact or immersion in water. It also has an independent power source that will emit an emergency signal for thirty days. The system is designed to enable the location of high-frequency sonar pings that are capable of being detected in deep water. Yet the CVR has not been recovered and no automatic emergency signals were ever picked up from it.

Flight data recorder. All technical information about the plane and its flight are automatically recorded by the flight data recorder; this means pilot's control inputs, electronic status, control surface positions, speed, altitude, a record of all geographical positions and other information that is helpful in finding a problem. Similarly, like the CVR, the FDR also has an emergency transmitter that is automatically activated by impact or submersion in water and it, too, has an independent power source that will continue to emit an emergency signal for thirty days after a crash. The system was also designed to enable the location of high-frequency sonar pings that are capable of being detected in deep waters. Like the three emergency locator transmitters, the cockpit voice recorder, the flight data recorder, no automatic emergency distress signals were ever picked up from any of them. *That's* an extremely *unlikely* occurrence.

Primary flight control computers. There is a system of nine computers that run a Boeing 777. The model is so advanced that it coordinates for its planes the altitudes at which they fly, their advance navigational way points, even possible alternate routes for their journeys. These are information programmed into the flight director's computers before the planes even take off. The Boeing 777 has three flight control computers, each with three independent channels for a total of nine computers, the majority of which must agree on their control outputs. How the software, hardware, and power supplies are isolated and integrated is a great technological advance. So even if one computer fails, others are running. The flight computer is programmed to handle the failure of various parts of the airplane. For instance, in the case of a partial electrical failure, it must determine what components or functions are to be shut down and in what order.

The multiple safeguards design is also employed in the electrical systems of the plane by the electrical load management sys- tem (ELMS). The ELMS manages the aircraft's electrical loads and the protection of all of the aircraft's electrical systems to ensure that power is always available to the critical equipment that needs it. The power system's reliability is very high, and there are numerous ways power can be switched between busses, depending upon the type of failure and what power is available from which source. Even in the event of total electrical failure, the systems on board the aircraft would be able to continue to operate and it could continue to fly. In other words, the idea that one problem or a bad decision from someone could knock the plane out of the sky is unlikely and unrealistic. Furthermore, the programming of the flight control computers is done by inputs from the pilots, the automatic pilot system, the auto land control, and the flight director programs and controls other systems.

The flight control computers control the functions of the air- craft during the flight. In addition, the fly-by-wire system is a new system that eliminates the direct connections between the pilot and the aircraft controls. It does so by using electrical inputs that bypass the flight crew and go directly into the flight control computer. The Boeing website explains, "The flight control system for the 777 air- plane is different from those on other Boeing airplane designs. As a result, the 777 uses wires to carry electrical signals from the pilot control wheel. The pilot has the ability to override the flight control computer systems, if they choose to in the event of an emergency. The flight computers can fly a plane without the pilots. They have the capability. However, the 777 incorporates inputs from the flight crew to avoid the potential dangers of too automated a flight system."

In the Boeing 777, the pilot oversees the various processes during flight and the landing is the result of inputs by the flight crew. The Boeing 777 is a highly sophisticated aircraft that can itself operate the flight functions of the plane, even prioritizing systems when problems arise and always determining the safest and most secure manner in which to proceed. The survivability of the aircraft is built-in by design. Actually, as of March 8, 2014, the survivability of the Boeing 777 had been tested and proven over a period of nineteen years.

Automatic fire and smoke suppression systems. Smoke detectors and fire suppression systems are located throughout the Boeing 777 aircraft. Each of the plane's three cargo compartments is equipped with smoke detection systems. There is a system in place to automatically address smoke and fire.

Cockpit security. The door to the cockpit of a Boeing 777 meets security standards for ballistics because it's bulletproof and intruder resistant. It locks automatically, electrically, and has a manual lock as well.

Electronics equipment bay. The electronics equipment bay, as it is known, contains all the electrical systems of the aircraft and is located underneath the cockpit. The Boeing 777 is designed to automatically restore electrical systems after a power surge.

Emergency oxygen supply. The emergency supply system in the cockpit is more sophisticated than that of the passenger cabin. It is designed to get the pilots through a decompression or a fire so that they can control the plane. The experts said the pilots' oxygen masks have an inflatable head harness for a quick, snug fit. The pilots' masks prevent breathing of smoke or noxious gasses and must be set at 100 percent oxygen. If smoke is present, the amount of oxygen must allow at least twelve minutes of oxygen which is enough time to get the airplane down to 10,000 feet on most routes.

Emergency doors are very safe. You cannot open the doors or emergency hatches of an airplane in flight; the cabin pressure won't allow it.

Bulletproof elements. If a bullet simply punctures the skin of the airplane, no problem. The cabin of the airplane is pressurized and the hole creates a small leak, but the pressurization system will compensate for it. A single hole or even a few holes like this will have no effect.

CHAPTER VI

The Disappearance of Malaysian Airlines Flight #370

"Any sufficiently advanced technology would appear indistinguishable from magic."

—Arthur C. Clarke
(12/16/1917–3/19/2008)

"I've often wondered, what if all of us in the world discovered that we were threatened by a power from outer space, from another planet, would we all of a sudden find that we didn't have differences between us all?"

—Former US President Ronald Reagan
(2/6/1911–6/5/2004)

On March 8, 2014, Malaysian Airlines Flight #370 departed Kuala Lumpur airport in Malaysia at 12:41 a.m. to Beijing, China. The plane was expected to arrive at 6:30 a.m. The plane carried 227 passengers and twelve crew members.

Timeline of Flight #370

12:41 a.m.: Flight #370 operated by Malaysia Airlines leaves Kuala Lumpur International Airport bound for Beijing, China, with 227 passengers, of whom two-thirds are Chinese and a Malaysian crew of twelve.

1:07 a.m.: The aircraft communications addressing and reporting system or ACARS, which transmits data about the plane's performance, sends a scheduled message. The next one is scheduled for 1:37 a.m.

1:19 a.m.: Someone in the cockpit, believed to be the copilot, makes the last voice contact with ground control, saying, "All right, good night."

1:21 a.m.: The plane's transponder, which broadcasts its identity, altitude, and speed, stops working.

After 1:21 a.m.: The plane turns off course and heads west. The turn is not executed manually using cockpit controls. Shockingly, it is entered into a cockpit computer sometime before or after take-off. As a result, investigators believe that the plane was deliberately diverted.

1:37 a.m.: ACARS fails to send a scheduled message which suggests that it has been *shut off* or has failed sometime in the past half-hour.

2:15 a.m.: The plane is detected by military radar flying west. It ascends to 45,000 feet, above limit for a Boeing 777, then descends unevenly to 23,000 feet, and eventually flies out over the Indian Ocean.

7:24 a.m.: Malaysian Airlines announces that it has lost contact with the aircraft, about one hour before it was scheduled to arrive in Beijing.

8:11 a.m.: The plane sends hourly signals to a satellite, suggesting that it was still intact and flying. Malaysian authorities say it had enough fuel to keep flying for perhaps a half hour after the last signal received at 8:11.

The possible route. The only location information can be determined only from the plane's last signal received by the satellite. The possible location of the plane and last *ping* picked up by the satellite is centered along a circle. Obviously, parts of the location can be eliminated if it is too far from the plane. Also, the circle goes through areas where radar coverage would have detected the plane. The plane stopped communication with air traffic controllers and turned far off course, cutting back across peninsular

Malaysia, over the Strait of Malacca and toward the Indian Ocean. Military radar tracked it for a while, but the operators did not seek to identify the plane or alert anyone.

Actually, Malaysian investigators had identified two giant arcs of territory of the possible position of the plane, after the plane flew for about seven and a half hours after takeoff. This is based on its last faint signal to a satellite, an hourly *handshake* signal that continues even when communications are switched off. The arcs stretch up as far as Kazakhstan in Central Asia and down deep into the southern Indian Ocean. A satellite orbiting at 22,250 miles above the earth over the middle of the Indian Ocean received the last *ping* trans- mission from the plane seven and a half hours after it took off from Kuala Lumpur airport.

The other arc runs northern through Thailand, Jakarta, and the Indian Ocean, roughly 1,000 miles off the west coast of Australia. Malaysian authorities stated, "The plane changed course after it took off. The movements are consistent with deliberate action by some- one on the plane." Also, they said, "One communication system had been disabled as the plane flew over the northeast coast of Malaysia." A second system abruptly stopped broadcasting its location, altitude, speed, and other information at 1:21 a.m. while the plane was a third of the way across the Gulf of Thailand from Malaysia to Vietnam. However, military radar showed that the plane turned and flew west across northern Malaysia before arcing out over the wide northern end of the Strait of Malacca, headed for the Indian Ocean.

A blip unidentified. Military radar operators reported an unidentified blip or aircraft at several points, apparently headed west across the Malaysian peninsula and out into the Indian Ocean. The head of the country's air force told reporters the military took no immediate action to investigate the unidentified blips. The path appeared to take the aircraft near the heavily populated island of Penang. The search area was then expanded into waters west and east of the pen- insula, encompassing almost 27,000 square nautical miles, an area bigger than South Carolina. The military declined to offer an explanation for the coincidence of an unidentified *blip* suddenly appearing on military radar screens after Flight #370 stopped transmitting its identification signal to civilian ground controllers forty minutes into its flight. The military said, "Today we are still not sure that it is the same aircraft." See Case 8, the Kinross plane disappearance on November 23, 1953. The radars pick up an unidentified *blip* over a restricted area. So a plane was sent to investigate with Capt. Felix Moncla Jr. The plane and pilot were taken and never seen again.

The Malaysian authorities stated that the aircraft's communications systems were systematically disabled, perhaps by someone with a very good knowledge of the plane. They said that one system was disabled as the plane flew over the northeast coast of Malaysia and that a second transponder was disabled a few minutes later. The aircraft then altered course and flew over the Malaysian mainland before turning to the northwest and heading out to the open sea. Also, the Malaysian authorities said that someone may have piloted the aircraft to as high as 45,000 feet above the 43,100-foot ceiling for the Boeing 777. An expert pilot stated that the move could have been intended to depressurize the cabin and render the passengers and crew unconscious, preventing them from alerting people on the ground with their cellphones. "Incapacitate them so as to carry on your plan uninterrupted."

White House spokesman Jay Carney stated, "Authorities searching for the plane may expand the search into the Indian Ocean which extends hundreds of miles farther west." The Obama administration said new information received points that the plane's engines remained running for approximately four hours after it vanished from radar which came from satellite signals or a *ping*. This belief was based on satellite data, not signals from monitoring systems embedded in the plane's Rolls-Royce engines. According to senior American officials, the first turn to the west that diverted Flight #370 from its route from Kuala Lumpur to Beijing was carried out through a computer system that was most likely programmed by someone in the plane's cockpit who was knowledgeable about airplane systems. Instead of manually operating the plane's controls, they claim that whoever altered Flight #370's path typed seven or eight keystrokes into a computer on a knee-high pedestal between the captain and the first officer.

According to Malaysian authorities, the flight management system, as the computer is known, directs the plane from point to point specified in the flight plan submitted before a flight. It is not clear whether the plane's path was reprogrammed before or after it took off. Furthermore, air traffic control radar, a close reading of the report indicates the autopilot could have been on as early as one hour after the plane was off course. In case of a loss of oxygen, the emergency masks in the cockpit should have provided about an hour of oxygen if everything was operating properly. On the other hand, passengers had less than twenty minutes, according to air safety experts. Malaysian radars tracked the plane as it flew west across the northern peninsula of Malaysia, making a couple of turns before disappearing toward the northern end of the Indonesian island of Sumatra. Automatic pings transmitted by the plane's engines to a satellite over the Indian Ocean showed that the engine operated for six more hours.

The electronic handshake *or digital communication between the airplane and a satellite orbiting 22,250 miles above the Indian Ocean.* The satellite is in a geosynchronous orbit. In other words, it seems to hang in a fixed spot above the earth. However, the handshake doesn't provide data about the location of the plane. The only thing it does is to establish the angle between the satellite and the plane. Investigators have concluded that Flight #370 remained in controlled flight for at least six hours after contact was lost, until it ran out of fuel over the southern Indian Ocean. Also, investigators believed that Flight #370 flew for hours on autopilot. Similarly, Australian authorities believed that someone on board the plane switched on the autopilot system *deliberately* after the plane turned toward the southern Indian Ocean. Additionally, they believe that all 239 passengers and crew had become unresponsive—possible after being deprived of oxygen—before the plane ran out of fuel and crashed in the Indian Ocean. Likewise, investigators believed that human intervention took control of the plane toward one of the most remote parts of the planet. Also, they can answer what might have caused the oxygen depletion known as hypoxia. They assumed that theory because the plane traveled for about five hours without any communication, turns, or deviation and no altitude change, and that Flight #370 ended up crashing in the Indian Ocean after it ran out of fuel.

·

Nevertheless, highly sensitive infrasonic atmospheric sensors can pick up sound waves from a wide variety of sources, including rocket launches and aircraft crashes. Infrasonic data are constantly monitored by a watchdog agency of the United Nations. The reason is to watch for nuclear explosions and missile launches. The Comprehensive Nuclear-Test-Ban Treaty Organization (CTBTO) said that they can detect explosions and impacts of aircraft on water. Furthermore, the spokesman for UN Secretary General Ban Ki-Moon, Stephane Dujarric, told reporters in New York on March 17, nine days after Flight #370 disappeared, that "The Vienna-based Comprehensive Nuclear-Test-Ban Treaty Organization (CTBTO) confirmed that neither an *explosion* nor a *plane crash* on *land* or on *water* had been *detected* so far."

CHAPTER VII
The Search for Flight #370

"In the firm belief that the American public deserves a better explanation than thus far given by the Air Force, I strongly recommend that there be a committee investigation of the UFO phenomenon."

—Former US President Gerald Ford,
1966 (July 14, 1913–)

T he Malaysian officials said, "The possible northern corridor described bristles with military radar, making it more likely that the plane either went south or the plane flew north." Another official said, "If they had taken the northern corridor, they could have gone down before they reached land." The two corridors were theoretical possible trajectories, according to calculations by engineers from the satellite communications company Inmarsat, which were provided to investigators. In fact, investigators have managed to calculate the distance between the *ping* from the plane and a stationary Inmarsat-3 satellite. "The satellite can see in an arc that stretches north and south of its fixed position, but without GPS it can say only how far away the ping is, not where it is coming from," said the investigator. However, based on what is known about the flight's trajectory, investigators are strongly favoring the southern corridor as the most likely as the flight path. The *ping* picked up by the satellite creates a range of possible locations along the edge of a circle centered on the satellite.

In addition, a senior military official said investigators were focusing more on the southern arc because of a lack of evidence that the plane had flown over land. Further, twenty-six countries, among them China, Australia, France, the US, and other nations, have offered ships, surveillance planes, satellites, and experts in maritime disasters. According to officials, the plane was about forty minutes into a six-hour trip to Beijing from Kuala Lumpur, the Malaysian capital, early on March 8 when it suddenly stopped communicating with air traffic controllers and turned far off course, cutting back across peninsular Malaysia, over the Strait of Malacca, and toward the Indian Ocean. In addition, the United States had two destroyers, the *Kid* and the *Pinckney*, that continued to patrol the eastern waters along with ships from China, Malaysia, Vietnam—twenty-six countries in total. In all, forty-two ships and thirty-nine aircraft were taking part in the search operation. Furthermore, after fifty-three days of fruitless search, Australia, Malaysia, and China began a search of the ocean floor.

Australian officials said in early May 2014 that twenty-nine planes and fourteen ships scanned nearly 1.8 million square miles of ocean, an area nearly three times the size of Alaska. But no debris was found. Moreover, a Bluefin-21 autonomous submersible combed 328 square miles of ocean floor where the pings were heard. The US Navy, which leased the sub, pulled it from the mission on May 28 without finding anything. Next, the Chinese ship *Zhu Kezhen* mapped 23,000 square miles of ocean floor, an area the size of West Virginia. Interestingly, there are 80,000 commercial flights per day with Western-built aircraft, according to IATA. Australian officials said that scouring the ocean floor will cost $60 million. The nearly three-year-long effort to find the missing jet cost $160 million, the largest and most expensive search in aviation history. The search scoured 46,000 square miles of the Indian Ocean and the seabed.

The governments of China, Malaysia, and Australia, which together have conducted the search for the missing plane, concluded that the plane had crashed within a vast area of the Indian Ocean north, but no wreckage had been found. Further, more than 1.8 million square miles of ocean were searched without any luck in finding debris. The authorities never received distress calls or Maydays from Flight #370. Also, no reports of threatening weather. No clue that a crash had even taken place. The three-year search for Flight #370 will be suspended, the three countries conducting the operation announced. They stated, "In the absence of new evidence, Malaysia, Australia, and China have collectively decided to stop what is already the most expensive search in aviation history, having cost 180 million Australian dollars" upon completion of the 120,000 square kilometers (46,300 square miles). In fact, Malaysian officials describe it as an unprecedented aviation mystery. It remains unknown whether the plane crashed on land or in the ocean.

Similarly, the US officials said they did not know what direction the plane flew or whether it simply circled during the approximately four hours or whether it was airborne at all. However, everything indicated that the plane ended in the Indian Ocean. "A large commercial airliner going missing without a trace for so long is unprecedented in modern aviation," said the International Air Transport Association. A relative of one of the passengers said, "Awful strange, no wreckage has been found since the plane disappeared." Investigators have concluded that Flight #370, which veered off course and disappeared, was probably not seriously damaged in the air and remained in con- trolled flight for hours until it ran out of fuel and crashed over the southern Indian Ocean. Furthermore, the sonar search of the ocean floor hasn't found any debris from the airliner. No wreckage, no oil slick, no debris from the plane had been found.

CHAPTER VIII

Current Theories about the Disappearance of Malaysian Airlines Flight #370

"In any case, the significance of UFOs may be that our fate is in the hands of beings from elsewhere for good or ill. If so, their powers and abilities are being made known to us, one might say, but their minds and thoughts remain shrouded in mystery. If UFOs carry advanced beings from another civilization in space, they may well be a sword of Damocles poised over our heads."

—Richard Hall, UFO scholar
(12/25/1930–7/17/2009)

Terrorism? The FBI and law enforcement conducted a very rigorous investigation of the passengers of the plane after officials in Rome and Vienna confirmed that the names of an Italian and an Austrian on the passenger list were traveling with stolen passports. The passports had been stolen in Thailand by two Iranians who wanted to escape an oppressive government. Furthermore, using a system that looks for flaws around the world, the Pentagon reviewed preliminary surveillance data from the area where the plane disappeared and saw no evidence of an explosion. Also, the Vienna-based Comprehensive Nuclear-Test-Ban Treaty Organization confirmed that "neither an explosion nor a plane crash on land or on water had been detected," said Stephane Dujarric, spokesperson for United Nations

Secretary General Ban Ki-Moon. According to law enforcement regarding the stolen passports, "At the time, we have not identified this as an act of terrorism." Also, they said, "While the stolen passports are interesting, they don't necessarily say to us that this was a terrorism act."

Additionally, a European counterterrorism official said that the Italian man whose passport was stolen—whose name is Luigi Maraldi, age thirty-seven—called his parents from Thailand where he was vacationing, eventually discovering that someone with his name was listed in the passenger list of Flight #370. Similarly, the Austrian passport—his name is Christian Korel, age thirty—was stolen two years before 2014. The Malaysian spokesman said that the plane had 227 passengers aboard, including two toddlers, a crew of Malaysians of twelve, 154 citizens of China, 38 Malaysian, seven Indonesian, six Australians, five Indians, four French, three Americans, two each from Canada and New Zealand and Ukraine, and one each from Austria, Italy, the Netherlands, and Russia.

As a matter of fact, the FBI and law enforcement checked the background of the passengers and they didn't find anything that could cause concern. All the passengers and crew were regular folks who lived normal lives. For instance, there was a passenger who gave his watch and wedding ring to his wife to give to their son, in case something happened to him. I wonder if this was a precognition. Also, it is a mystery that there were no phone calls. When the plane turned back into the Strait of Malacca, the plane was close to land. Furthermore, the crew was investigated.

The pilots. The copilot was only a few years out of flight school and still living at home with his family. The pilot was a grandfather and veteran pilot widely respected by colleagues and his community. His passion was to fly, cooking, and repairing his house. The two men lived ordinary lives. The captain, Zaharie Ahmad Shah, was fifty-three years old, and the first officer was Fariq Abdul Hamid, twenty-seven years old. Family and friends of the two men couldn't believe that they had something to do with the disappearance of Flight #370. A member of the Malaysian Parliament said, "Quite unthinkable. He was a very likable, very sociable kind of guy."

Likewise, relatives, friends, and colleagues have lined up in the pilot's defense and the copilot.

Mr. Zaharie lived a good life. He lived in a gated community. He was well-to-do and was a member of the political party. Furthermore, among Malaysian aviators, Mr. Zaharie had a reputation for professionalism and was regarded by the younger pilots as a mentor. Their opinion was "a very nice guy, passionate about aviation, and among the community of pilots, one of the most respected." Capt. Zaharie was a well-known participant in several online forums dedicated to flight simulation. He was so passionate about flight simulation that he built himself a simulator in his home and would invite friends and fellow pilots over to play with it. In addition, in January 2013, he joined the People's Justice Party because he was concerned about his country. Moreover, the younger pilot, Mr. Fariq, was less known in Kuala Lumpur, and on social media, he was middle class and had a girlfriend. He was also very well liked among friends and coworkers.

Suicide? This is a very unlikely possibility for all the reasons explained about these two men.

Weather? According to the weather report, the weather was fair and no distress signals or Mayday was received before the plane disappeared. As a matter of fact, the plane's systems were gradually switched off. That seems to rule out a sudden catastrophe, midair collision, or explosion.

Hijacking? Obviously, the terrorists don't have supernatural powers to disappear a peanut, much less an airplane the size of Flight #370. The Malaysian authorities thought that Flight #370 was hijacked because the transponders were switched off one by one after the plane flew in the northern arc and flew through the world's most volatile countries that are controlled by insurgent groups. Similarly, Flight #370 flew over areas with a strong military presence and air defense networks, some controlled by the American military. The northern arc passes close to northern Iraq, through Afghanistan, northern Pakistan, northern India. These countries are heavily defended, also the Himalayas and Myanmar. Flight #370, if it had traveled to these locations, would had been seen. Furthermore, the United States and NATO countries have bases in Afghanistan; for instance, Bagram Airfield, where the United States Air Force has the 455th Air Expeditionary Wing.

Indeed, it is impossible for Flight #370 to have flown, much less crashed, in any of these countries, or be hijacked because we will know immediately. Furthermore, the Pentagon and the Vienna-based Comprehensive Nuclear-Test-Ban Treaty Organization confirmed that "neither an explosion nor a plane crash on land or on water had been detected." So terrorism and hijacking have to be discarded as possible causes of the disappearance of Flight #370.

Flight #370 was in autopilot? The plane was not in autopilot. The reason is that there was not a reason for an experienced pilot like Capt. Zaharie to put the plane in autopilot. I will explain in the next chapter.

Flight #370 hijacked to the military base in the island of Diego Garcia? Obviously, the answer is no. Diego Garcia is an American base and Boeing is an American company. The American military has no need to steal secrets from an American company.

The unidentified blimp? The Malaysian military never have identified the blimp. Probably it was a UFO? *Debris?* Interestingly, it was a theory that two pieces of a Boeing 777 found in the Indian Ocean probably came from Flight #370. The two pieces of debris—part of a wing and a piece of tail section— were found about 130 miles and eight weeks apart along the coast of Mozambique in southeast Africa, although this area is thousands of miles from Flight #370's believed crash site. Moreover, on July 29, 2015 a *flaperon* was discovered in the island of Reunion. Likewise, at least half a dozen objects have been discovered that some people claimed came from Flight #370. The problem is that the Pentagon and the Vienna Nuclear-Test-Ban Treaty Organization stated that "neither an explosion nor a plane crash on land or on water had been detected." Furthermore, many parts of the plane are naturally buoyant and if crashed in the ocean, it will float. In other cases of planes crashing in the ocean, debris has been spotted floating on the surface of the water. For instance, seat cushions float. Also, many nonmetallic aircraft parts will be massive debris floating in the ocean; it will be very easy to spot.

Missile? The missile would have left a radar signature, and again there are no debris or wreckage to support the theory that a missile shot down Flight #370. Certainly, there is no evidence of an explosion or crash on land or water, as I explained before.

A fire in Flight #370? Moreover, another theory as a possible cause for the disappearance of Flight #370 is there probably was an onboard fire that caused the disappearance of Flight #370. Surely, we see fires every day in houses, cars, etc. Do the objects on fire dis- appear? Obviously, the answer is no and the same applies to Flight #370. Some experts suggest that a fire may have been started by an overheated tire on the front landing gear. Actually, another expert said, "It would be unprecedented for a fire to start, take out the flight deck crew, take out the radio, ACARS, and the transponder and then for the fire to stop or be extinguished, and then for the aircraft to continue on flying for hours." Nonetheless, Flight #370 had automatic fire and smoke suppression systems which are located through- out the Boeing 777. Also, each of the plane's three cargo compartments is equipped with smoke detection. In addition, a Boeing 777 is designed to autonomously restore electrical systems after power surges without human intervention. Obviously, the total absence of debris, wreckage, oil slick, buoyant objects from the plane, like seat cushions, luggage, etc., made this theory impossible.

Mechanical failure? This is another assumption by experts that probably a mechanical failure caused the plane to disappear. Obviously, the answer is no for all the reasons mentioned previously.

A military exercise was taking place during Flight #370's disappearance? By the same token, there are some rumors that two huge joint military exercises were taking place at the same time that Flight #370 vanished from radar. Although, if true, the media never reported this event. At least, I never saw or read it in the newspaper. Indeed, it is shocking that the countries that were present in the military exercises—the United States, Thailand, Singapore, and other countries—were observers of the annual exercise *Cobra Gold* and *Cape Tiger*. The exercises began on February 11 and ended on March 21, 2014. The military Air Forces of the United States, Singapore, and Thailand's Navy, also South Korea, Japan, and Malaysia were present, an investigator said, "The fact that the plane disappeared from radar without warning indicated there was something unprecedented that hasn't happened before."

Sabotage? Another theory is that probably someone sabotaged the plane. Experts have been baffled how a large passenger jet like Flight #370 seems to have flown undetected by military radars for up to six hours. On the other hand, the failure of the air and sea search to find any wreckage around Flight #370's last known location suggests a bomb did not bring down Flight #370.

In summary, none of the current theories explained here provide a satisfactory answer to the mystery. The cockpit voice recorder, the flight data recorder, the three ELTs are automatically activated by a crash on water or land. The Pentagon and the Vienna-based Comprehensive Nuclear-Test-Ban Treaty Organization didn't detect any explosion or crash on land or water. I think the only explanation is that the plane was unfortunately teleported.

CHAPTER IX

What Really Happened to Malaysian Airlines Flight #370

"If despite this still unclarified possibility, the extraterrestrial origin of the saucers should be confirmed, this would prove the existence of intelligent interplanetary communication. What such a fact might mean for humanity cannot be imagined but there is no doubt we should find ourselves in the same critical situation as primitive societies confronted with the superior culture of man. The reign of power would be wrenched from our hands, and as an old witch doctor once told me with tears in his eyes, 'We would have no dreams anymore.' The lofty flights of our spirit would have been checked and crippled forever. Naturally, the first thing to be considered consigned to the rubbish heap would be our science and technology. What the moral effects of such a catastrophe would be can be seen from the pitiless decay of primitive cultures taking place before our eyes. That the construction of such machines would be evidence of a scientific technology immensely superior to ours admits of no two opinions. Just as the Pax Britannica put an end to tribal warfare in Africa, so our world could run up its iron and use it as so much scrap along with all the billions of armaments, warships, and munitions. That wouldn't be such a bad thing but we would have been discovered and colonized—reason enough for universal panic. If we wish to avoid such catastrophe, the officials in possession of authoritative information should not hesitate to enlighten the public as speedily and thoroughly as possible, and above all this stupid game of mystification and suggestive allusion. Instead they have allowed a lot of fantastic and mendacious publicity to run riot, the best possible preparation for panic and psychic epidemics."

—Dr. Carl G. Jung (1875–1961)

"Receiving a visit from outer space seems almost as comfortable as having a God. Yet we shouldn't rejoice too soon. Perhaps we will get the visitors we deserve."

—Dr. Jacques Valle, UFO Scholar

"We have learned that we cannot regard this planet as being fenced in a secure abiding place, we can never anticipate the unseen good or evil that may come upon us suddenly out of space."

—H. G. Wells (9/21/1866–8/13/1946)

On March 8, 2014, Malaysian Airlines Flight #370 departed Kuala Lumpur airport in Malaysia at 12:41 a.m., expecting to arrive to Beijing, China, at 6:30 a.m.

Phase (1) 1:07 a.m.: The aircraft communications addressing and reporting system, or ACARS, which transmits data about the plane's performance, sends a scheduled message. The next one is schedule at 1:37 a.m.

1:19 a.m.: Someone in the cockpit, believed to be the copilot, makes the last voice recorder contact with ground control, saying, "All right, good night." Similarly, in many cases of teleportation of planes, ships, and people, the last message had been normal, without any signs of a tragic end. For instance, the DC3, a chartered passenger plane approaching Miami for a landing, the pilot announced, "We are approaching Miami for a landing. We are approaching the field. We can see the lights of Miami now. Will stand by for landing instructions." After this message, the plane disappeared, and no debris, wreckage, oil slick, or bodies were found. Similarly, the Star Tiger plane's last message was "Weather and performance excellent.

Expect to arrive on schedule." After this message, the plane disappeared, and no debris, wreckage, oil slick, or bodies were found. By the same token, the famous yacht-racing Harvey Conover sent a cheerful last message, approaching the yacht club that he will arrive "in forty-five minutes. Save a place at the bar." He never was found nor his yacht.

The disappearance of Flight #19 was different. It seems to me that the intelligence behind the UFO phenomenon affected the cognitive mental process to take or follow with the abduction process. The pilot said, "We don't know which way is west. Everything is wrong...strange. We can't be sure of any direction, even the ocean doesn't look as it should." After this message, five planes vanished and the sixth one that went to look for them. No wreckage, oil slick, or debris were found. Moreover, Amelia Earhart's last message was, "We cannot see you, gas running low. We must be over you. We cannot see you. We are circling you. We cannot hear you." The weather was excellent in these two cases. She was close to the *Itasca* but couldn't see. The UFO phenomenon can change the surroundings before the abduction takes place.

Phase (2) 1:21 a.m.: The plane's transponder, which broadcasts its identity, altitude, and speed, stops working. See chapter 5 where I explained the functions of the transponders. Similarly, the three computers are turned off. Read Case 2. In a similar form, the transponder and computers were turned off in Flight #370.

Phase (2) 1:21 a.m.: The plane changes course and heads to the Indian Ocean. Read Cases 3 and 4. This is the way Flight #370 was kidnapped. It seems to me that the pilots, crew, and passengers were put in a trance. That is the reason there were no phone calls from the passengers or two pilots.

Phase (3): Surely, after the transponders and computers were off and the passengers and crew were in a trance, Flight #370 was taken on a form of joyride through the Indian Ocean in the same form that took place in Cases 3 and 4. Obviously, Flight #370 did not explode or crash in land or the ocean. An investigator of the disappearance of Flight #370 said, "The inescapable conclusion is that Flight #370 simply vanished in some way that we do not yet understand." Also, investigators said, "How, in this high-tech age of over surveillance in which hundreds of satellites sweep the Earth and modern air- craft have multiple communications systems, can a plane vanish?" Certainly, this is a very unusual form the way Flight #370 was tele- ported. As I have shown in the first three chapters, teleportation is a total and sudden phenomenon that takes place without warning. Certainly, the Vienna- based Comprehensive Nuclear-Test-Ban Treaty Organization confirmed that "neither an explosion nor a plane crash on land or on water had been detected." Also, the Pentagon con- firmed no detection of an explosion in the Indian Ocean.

Furthermore, the transponders and the ELTs, or the emergencies locator transmitters, and the cockpit recorder and the flight data recorder are activated when in contact with water or hard surfaces. Obviously, the plane didn't crash on land or in the Indian Ocean. The debris that Australia claimed belonged to Flight #370 is in contradiction with the previous statements because there is no evidence of an explosion or crash in land or the ocean.

The plane was taken on a joyride into the Indian Ocean, and then teleported. Why the intelligence behind the UFO phenome- non chose to take the plane in this form is unknown. For instance, Flight #19 was taken suddenly and without any warnings. I have been researching UFOs for thirty years and this is the first time I saw something like the case of Flight #370. Actually, according to some information, the flight crew of two commercial airliners flying near Flight #370 were asked to radio communicate with Flight #370 and did so, receiving only a garbled response. This can be one clue to teleportation.

In other information, the *China Times* reported that on March 8, 2014, Flight #370 made a distress call that they wanted to land because the *cabin faced disintegration*. The distress call was recorded by a US Navy listening post. The US Embassy handed over the tape recordings to the Malaysian government. However, this has not been confirmed by any of the governments involved in the search for Flight #370. However, if it is the truth, this confirms that the intelligence behind the UFO phenomenon teleported Flight #370. Furthermore, the number of cell phone rings from a jet liner as large as Flight #370 would be easy to listen to with the high-tech listening stations the United States has around the world. The plane could not be located via those digitized signals. Unfortunately, Flight #370 was teleported out of this planet. Probably we will never know where it is located.

CHAPTER X

Where Are the People and Planes Teleported by the Intelligence Behind the UFO Phenomenon?

"As a reliable compass for orientating yourself in life, nothing is more useful than to accustom yourself to regarding this world as a place of atonement, a sort of penal colony. When you have done this, you will order your expectations of life according to the nature of things and no longer regard the calamities, sufferings, torments, and miseries of life as something irregular and not to be expected but will find them entirely in order, well knowing that each of us is here being punished for his existence and each in his own particular way."

—Arthur Schopenhauer (1788–1860)

"Nothing in fact—neither wild beast nor microbes—can be more terrible for man than a species that is intelligent, flesh- eating, cruel; a species which would be able to understand and to thwart the human intelligence; a species whose goal would be precisely the destruction of man. That species is obviously ours."

—Jean-Paul Sartre, French Philosopher
(1905–1980)

According to reports in New Jersey, the missing bureau reported in 2000 19,955 people missing. Likewise, the missing bureau reported in 2001 20,223 people missing. Furthermore, in 2002, 19,354. In

2003, 19,893. In 2004, 18,893. In 2005, 18,620. In 2006, 13,208 people missing. In fact, the number of active unsolved missing people's cases since 2001 are 1,691. In the US, about 95 percent return; the remaining 5 percent vanish forever. Actually 75 percent to 80 percent of reported missing persons are juveniles. According to some researchers, approximately from 100,000 to 10,000,000 people go missing every year in the United States alone. So how many people go missing around the world? I will say in the couple of millions. Obviously, a large percentage of people are found, and others voluntarily disappear for many reasons. Some voluntarily disappear for economic, family, or emotional reasons. Conversely, the cases that I presented in the first three chapters are the most bizarre and out of the ordinary cases.

The late great UFO scholar Ivan T. Sanderson estimated that there were six Bermuda Triangles around the world. The first group is formed by the Bermuda Triangle and an area around the Mediterranean Sea. The second is off the coast of Japan. The third area is off the coast of Australia, Africa, and South America. Although, teleportation takes place anywhere and everywhere in malls, around the house, country roads, at the house garden, everywhere. Certainly, teleportation is taking place 24/7 around the world. For no apparent reason, people just disappear off the face of the Earth and are never seen again. What is the fate of the people who are teleported? Obviously, there is no warning that you are going to be teleported. You don't get a letter that explains to you what is in store for you. When you are teleported, your fate is unknown. The evidence is that the intelligence behind the UFO phenomenon had been teleporting people since the beginning of history.

My question is why the intelligence behind the UFO phenomenon keeps teleporting humans since the beginning of history. A civilization that can teleport a plane as big as Flight #370 has mastered physics at the quantum level. Teleportation is the theoretical transfer of matter or energy from one point to another without traversing the physical space between them. The scientist Hans Christian stated, "But it would take an unbelievable amount of data processing. Even a coffee cup without the coffee would take many times the age of the universe." In other words, we would need a computer more super- powerful than any we have ever seen, a supercomputer that would enable simulations of physical processes at the quantum level. So the intelligence behind the UFO phenomenon with this technology can create life, move asteroids, and create universes. So, in other words, the intelligence behind the UFO phenomenon are like gods because they can create and recreate anything in the universe. So for what rea- son would they need to teleport or kidnap people from this planet? Probably the intelligence behind the UFO phenomenon knows that human greed, religious fanaticism, Jihadism, and Putinism are going to bring the end of human civilization. Probably, they are preparing another Earth and they need a vast supply of humans. Probably, we are part of a cosmic circus. Probably, they keep us as pets and guinea pigs. I am just speculating. Probably, we will never know the truth.

Furthermore, why doesn't the intelligence behind the UFO phenomenon teleport bad dictators and murderers, like Hitler, Stalin, Hirohito, past dictators, or present dictators like Assad, Putin, Maduro, Kim Jong-Un? Obviously, the answer is that the intelligence behind the UFO phenomenon is not here for the service of the majority of humankind but to serve their own purposes, whatever they may be. Certainly, the intelligence behind the UFO phenomenon should know more about us than we know about ourselves because they have been kidnapping humans for thousands of years. I hope they are not anthropophagy. Furthermore, the intelligence behind the UFO phenomenon may be testing out the state of the human mind to see when we will be ready to accept the shocking truth that we humans are a product-design of the intelligence behind the UFO phenomenon. After that, they will introduce us to the brotherhood of civilizations in the universe.

In summary, I hope that all the humans who had been tele- ported since the beginning of history are in a much better world—a world without human greed and, more importantly, without poverty.

CHAPTER XI

The Nature of Intelligence Behind the UFO Phenomenon

"UFOs have always been observed, they didn't signify anything. Now, suddenly, they seem to portend something because that something has been projected on them—a hope, an expectation. What sort of expectation you can see from the literature: It is of course the expectation of a savior. But that is only one aspect. There is another aspect, a mythological one. The UFO can be a ship of death, which means that ships of death are coming to fetch the living or to bring souls. Either these souls will fall into birth, or many people are going to die and will be fetched by fleets of these ships of death. These are important archetypal ideas because they can also be predictions. If an atomic war were to break out, an infinite multitude of souls would be carried away from the earth."

—Dr. Carl G. Jung (1875–1961)

O bviously, it is not an easy answer to define the nature of the intelligence behind the UFO phenomenon. The best thing we can do is to analyze the sightings and witness reports of claims of contact with alien beings. We have plenty of evidence of an alien presence in the planet. The first thing that UFO abductees report is that aliens and space- ships go through walls, ground, and solid matter. As a matter of fact, UFOs and the aliens that pilot them are not going through solid matter because of magic. They are going through solid matter because of a physical advanced technology. Conversely, the electromagnetic force, the strong nuclear force, and the weak nuclear force, every particle inter- acts through some combination of those forces. For instance, gravity affects everything with mass or energy. In addition to gravity, electrons feel the electromagnetic and weak nuclear forces. Actually, protons and neutrons interact through all four elementary forces. Ultimately, it is the strong nuclear force that holds quarks together to form protons and neutrons and holds protons and neutrons together inside of atoms in a compact nucleus. Certainly, the electromagnetic and strong nuclear forces are the two strongest forces of nature. It is these forces that make protons, neutrons, and electrons easy to detect and observe.

The reason your hand stops when you press it against a table is that the electric charge inside the table repels the electric charge in your hand. This is the result of the electromagnetic force. If this force were somehow turned off, your hand would simply pass through the table! For instance, in 1947, ten people in St. Maries, Idaho, reported that eight UFOs had landed near the mountainside. The witnesses said that they came into view at an extreme speed, suddenly slowed, and then fluttered like leaves to the ground. The ten people went to look for the UFOs that it seemed had crashed on the ground. Shockingly, it seems that the UFOs went *through* the ground. This is an example of how the UFO and aliens turned off the electromagnetic force. They couldn't find wreckage.

Moreover, the subject of UFOs is very broad, and people don't know that is the source of religion, supernatural phenomenon, folk- lore, and mythology. I have been researching UFOs for thirty years. My discoveries are in my first book, *The UFO Phenomenon and the Birth of the Jewish, Christian, and Muslim Religions*. In this book, I explained how the three major religions are products of the UFO phenomenon. Obviously, for the vast majority of people, *flying saucers* are only a modern myth, without any major consequence. Furthermore, the UFO phenomenon is the source of the supernatural phenomena known as ghosts, haunting, and poltergeists. In my book *A Treatise on Human Nature: Christian Saints, Historical Figures, and the UFO Phenomenon*, I explained why the UFO phenomenon is the source of the supernatural. Certainly, I was shocked during my research to discover that the UFO phenomenon is the source of the near-death experience and the out-of-body experience. The scary thing about this phenomenon is that it seems that our destiny and fate is pre- conceived by this phenomenon. According to numerous witnesses, aliens have been seen in human form and animal form. For instance, the famous *Chupacabra* is an alien in the form of a monster. Also, the aliens take the form of the so-called devil and ghosts.

Furthermore, all the myths and religious books are just historical records of the interaction of aliens and humans. The best example of interaction of aliens and humans is in the Bible. Likewise, there are approximately 70,000 sightings of UFOs per year. The list of UFO sightings goes back to the first Sumerian and Egyptian writ- ten records, all the way to 2017. In addition, there are astronomical UFO sightings that go back to the seventeenth century of gigantic objects in space crossing the orbits of the moon's disk and in movements that defy the laws of physics. Likewise, thousands of people disappear a year, without any good explanation. I wonder if we are dealing with a race of anthropophagic aliens.

The Bible is the richest source for interactions of aliens and humans; for example, the description of *chariots of fire* and *glowing clouds* with visitations of angels. Also the story that the sons of God took unto themselves wives from the daughters of earth. Additionally, since the beginning of history, there are major archaeological finds of hieroglyphics, carvings, and cave paintings from prehistoric times with spacecraft and astronaut like designs with no explanation about its origin; by the same token, the amazing feats of ancient engineering, pyramids all over the world—giant statues, colossal stone temples. Obviously, these wonders were impossible to build with Stone Age technology and an agricultural society. In fact, according to astronomers, there are at least one billion planets habitable in our galaxy along the Milky Way. So it is possible that the UFO phenomenon originates somewhere in our galaxy. Or maybe they are from another dimension. I think it is very possible the UFO phenomenon has mastered faster-than-light speeds, like teleportation for travel around the universe.

By the same token, there is the sudden appearance of civilizations like Sumerian, Egyptian, Mayans, and Aztecs with profound astronomical knowledge that without telescopes had advanced knowledge of the universe, also the Chaldeans with the mythological and religious legends of the *sky people* bringing knowledge to earth. Similarly, the amazing Piri Reis map copied from ancient charts that only UFOs could have made as early as 10,000 BC—the giant UFO landing fields observable only from the air, dating back to the beginning of history.

A great wave of UFOs was seen in 1947–1952 in the southwest near the atomic installations. It seems that the intelligence behind the UFO phenomenon are watching for the outbreak of the third world war. The waves of UFO sightings 1952-1957-1957-1961-1967-1973-1974 may be a preparation for the eventual appearance of the UFO phenomenon to the world. Furthermore, in my research I had found the possibility that the UFO phenomenon caused the origin of the Ice Ages and mass extinctions. In my next book coming soon, I will explain my theory.

Ultimately, in the introduction of this chapter, I introduced a theory of Dr. Jung. The first time I read it, I didn't think it possible, but now that I know more about the UFO phenomenon, I think it is very possible that the UFO phenomenon is waiting for the out- break of the third world war to *fetch the souls* to another dimension. Now science teaches us that what we call soul is nothing more than consciousness, experience, information. Now we know that that information can be extracted from the human brain. I think that is exactly what happens when we die, so the UFO phenomenon will be waiting for us at the end of human history. The UFO phenomenon is responsible for the near-death experiences and out-of-body experiences

Furthermore, according to witnesses, UFOs can penetrate the ground and solid walls. This is the effect of turning off the electro- magnetic force. Likewise, UFOs have been seen falling like leaves to the ground. The indentations produced by the UFOs in the ground, it seemed the objects weighed a couple of tons. So how can they fall like leaves? Also, witnesses have seen UFOs split into two and three objects. Moreover, some witnesses have seen UFOs take the form of planes. Similarly, UFOs are capable of joining in midair and vanishing. Also, they perform erratic sky dances, they perform dogfights, they can make themselves invisible, and they fly in zigzag. Similarly, the aliens that pilot the UFOs can become invisible and take human and animal form. Also, they can take the form of monsters like the Chupacabra or Bigfoot. According to UFO abductees, there are six- teen alien species on the planet. Also, UFO abductees claim that the aliens have bases underneath the oceans. The fact is that we don't know what is the nature of these UFO entities. Many witnesses have reported some aliens of a radioactive nature. Science should study more UFOs and inform the public because it will be too late when the invasion takes place and they appear as ghosts.

CONCLUSION

"What does it mean for a civilization to be a million years old? We have had radio telescopes and spaceships for a few decades; our technical civilization is a few hundred years old. An advanced civilization millions of years old is as much beyond us, as we are beyond a bush baby or macaque."

—Carl Sagan

"In the current scientific estimates, that's roughly8 billion. That's 8,000,000,000 potentially inhabitable systems exist in our galaxy alone."

—Ralph Blum, UFO Scholar

So, unfortunately, Flight #370 was teleported somewhere in the universe or into another dimension. What is the purpose of the intelligence behind the UFO phenomenon to teleport humans to their world? Probably, we will never know. The fact is that people are being teleported 24/7 around the world. In fact, no matter the age, race, social status, people are being teleported. For instance, in Case 92 in 96 AD, first-century philosopher and teacher known throughout the Roman Empire, Apollonius of Tyana, while he was walking was teleported. He was one hundred years old. So when people and the media said that somebody disappears, there are cases that defy human reason, and those are the cases that I present in this book.

Some cases are so bizarre, like Flight #370. My question is why past tyrants like Hitler, Stalin, Hirohito, and present tyrants like Assad, Kim Jong-Un, Putin, and Maduro aren't teleported. The answer is that the intelligence behind the UFO phenomenon is not here to save us from ourselves. They have their own agenda, whatever it is. The human race will have to find a way to save ourselves from our greed, religious fanaticism, imperialism, and totalitarianism.

So it seems that the intelligence behind the UFO phenomenon had been teleporting(kidnapping) people since the beginning of history, as we see in Case 92. I don't see a reason because a civilization that can teleport a plane as big as Flight #370 has mastered quantum physics. If they have mastered quantum physics, they can recreate anything because they can create matter from nothing. They can recreate anything at the quantum level. The UFO phenomenon can create anything, even life. So the intelligence behind the UFO phenomenon should be able to make copies of humans. Probably, we are part of a cosmic circus or we are taken as pets to different parts of the universe. Let's don't forget we are 98.4 percent sibling with the chimpanzee and cousin of the gorilla. Probably the aliens are taking people to a better world, better than the Republican Party that doesn't want to provide universal health care for the poor. The only thing we can do is to research more about UFOs and declare to the world that they are already here.

BIBLIOGRAPHY

- *The UFO Phenomenon and the Birth of the Jewish, Christian, and Muslim Religions* by Robert Iturralde
- *A Treatise on Human Nature: Christian Saints, Historical Figures, and the UFO Phenomenon* by Robert Iturralde
- *Essay on the Theory of the Earth: Electromagnetism in UFOs and the Origin of the Ice Ages and Mass Extinctions* by Robert Iturralde
- www.askthepilot.com
- www.governing.com
- www.usatoday.com
- http://gagettopia.com
- www.reuters.com/article
- www.cnn.com
- www.newsweek.com
- www.thewire.com
- www.forbes.com
- www.flyingmag.com
- www.huffingtonpost.com
- www.boeing.com/boeing/commercial/777 family/background/
- www.airliners.net/investigational/
- www.malaysiachronicle.com
- www.dccclothesline.com
- www.bbc.com/news
- www.slate.com
- www.theguardian.com
- www.nytimes.com

ABOUT THE AUTHOR

Robert Iturralde was a proud member of the United States Air Force and has been researching UFOs since 1987. The year when, by accident, he found a book about UFOs in a flea market. After reading the book, he went to the New York Times to check the reports of hundreds of witnesses; shockingly the reports were based in real eyewitness sightings. His previous three books are: *The UFO Phenomenon and the Birth of the Jewish, Christian and Muslim Religions*, *A Treatise on Human Nature: Christian Saints, Historical Figures and the UFO Phenomenon*, and *Essay on the Theory of the Earth: Electromagnetism in UFOs and the Origin of Mass Extinctions and the Ice Ages*. Mr. Iturralde is very active. He has participated in seventeen marathons, eleven triathlons and hundreds of running races. In his free time, he likes to play chess and run. If you have any questions about the book you can contact him through e-mail at Gastonterryatlas@gmail.com.

Printed in the United States
by Baker & Taylor Publisher Services